CRYSTALS FOR THE MIND

27 CRYSTALS, STONES, AND GEMS FOR ANXIETY AND STRESS

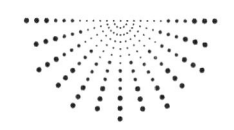

ALLEGRA GRANT

© **Copyright Allegra Grant 2021 - All rights reserved.**

The content contained within this book may not be reproduced, duplicated or transmitted without direct written permission from the author or the publisher.

Under no circumstances will any blame or legal responsibility be held against the publisher, or author, for any damages, reparation, or monetary loss due to the information contained within this book. Either directly or indirectly. You are responsible for your own choices, actions, and results.

Legal Notice:

This book is copyright protected. This book is only for personal use. You cannot amend, distribute, sell, use, quote or paraphrase any part, or the content within this book, without the consent of the author or publisher.

Disclaimer Notice:

Please note the information contained within this document is for educational and entertainment purposes only. All effort has been executed to present accurate, up to date, and reliable, complete information. No warranties of any kind are declared or implied. Readers acknowledge that the author is not engaging in the rendering of legal, financial, medical or professional advice. The content within this book has been derived from various sources. Please consult a licensed professional before attempting any techniques outlined in this book.

By reading this document, the reader agrees that under no circumstances is the author responsible for any losses, direct or indirect, which are incurred as a result of the use of the information contained within this document, including, but not limited to, — errors, omissions, or inaccuracies.

CONTENTS

Free Mini-Book Offer   v
Introduction   vii

1. WHAT ARE CRYSTALS, AND DO THEY ACTUALLY WORK?   1
2. CHOOSING YOUR CRYSTALS   16
3. 27 CRYSTALS FOR ANXIETY AND STRESS   41
   Root Chakra Crystals   44
   Sacral Chakra Crystals   51
   Solar Plexus Chakra Crystals   57
   Heart Chakra Crystals   62
   Throat Chakra Crystals   69
   Third Eye Chakra Crystals   74
   Crown Chakra Crystals   78
4. MODERN RITUALS   85
   Level 1: Easy does it   92
   Level 2: Getting a little fancypants   95
   Level 3: Being a little bit witchy with it   101
5. USING CRYSTALS TO SOOTHE YOUR STRESS AND ANXIETY   108
   Self-expression   109
   Digestive upset   110
   Overall wellness/Body care   112
   Self-doubt in relationships   116
   Difficulty sleeping   118
   Feeling tired or weak   119
   Negative thoughts   120
   Feeling agitated   121

Difficulty concentrating	121
Irritability	123
6. CARING FOR YOURSELF AND YOUR CRYSTALS	125

Conclusion	139
Resources	149
Notes	151

FREE MINI-BOOK OFFER

In THE COMPLETE GUIDE TO CLEANSING & CHARGING YOUR CRYSTALS, here's what you'll learn:

- Why you should care for your crystals
- A complete guide to Cleansing and Charging Methods
- My personal practices and why I cherish them

Go to www.AllegraGrant.com to get it NOW!

INTRODUCTION

THE DAY A BLUE ROCK (AND SOME RED WINE) CHANGED MY LIFE

"Let's go to the crystal shop!" Flora said.

"Uh, sure. Why not?" I was just drunk enough to agree.

It was one of those perfect Manhattan snowstorms: The commuters stay in New Jersey. The locals get an unexpected day off work. The city is beautiful and empty—a real snow-day for adults.

I already had plans with Flora to go for a glass of wine at happy hour, but "It's a snow-day! Let's just go now and spend the afternoon drinking and eating cheese." You had me at cheese.

Flora is one of those magnetic people—you know the type—edgy, confident, knows everything, makes you feel important even though you're an amoeba compared with her wit and vivacity...just the kind of person I slavishly adore.

Flora is cool. I'm...less so. I'm a practical girl. I do yoga. I write short stories that no one publishes. I enjoy baking and watching Netflix with my husband and our rescue dog, Cliff.

Flora and I were introduced by a mutual friend, Larissa, who throws a yearly Christmas party. We'd met there four years ago and looked forward to seeing each other every December. Or at least, I looked forward to seeing her! She is always so warm and welcoming. This day, in January, was the first time we'd ever hung out alone—just the two of us.

Flora, sporting a chic premature grey streak and blue highlights, is a former modern dancer. She's married to a highly sought-after tattoo artist, and she reads tarot cards at rich people's parties for extra money. In other words, she's way cooler than I could ever dream of being.

So, that snow-day, after many drinks, when she invited me to join her at the crystal store, of course, I said yes. I jumped at the chance, even though I privately thought crystals were, frankly, kind of dumb. I would be a good sport because it was Flora.

We walked into the surprisingly beautiful crystal shop—floor-to-ceiling display cases with piles of glittering...well, rocks. They were rocks. I was quietly skeptical. I also didn't want to spend real money on a crystal, because isn't it just a rock I'm going to put in a drawer?

Still, they were nice rocks; I had to admit that.

Besides the salesgirl, who was very quiet (and possibly very high?), it was just us in the store. Flora told me about her favorite crystals: the ones she keeps around her apartment, the ones she makes jewelry with, the ones she carries in her pocket for important events. She suggested I pick one out for myself. "Just look around and see which one is calling out to you!" (That statement would have seemed bonkers coming from anyone else, but again… it's Flora.)

Glancing at the thousands of multi-colored rocks, I thought, "Hey, why not? Maybe something magic is about to happen?" I have learned to appreciate that the world is full of things you can't possibly know for sure until you explore them.

I didn't believe in meditation until I tried it.

I didn't see the value in vegetarianism until I tried it. (And then gave it up, because bacon, but still…)

I didn't believe a New Yorker could effortlessly pull off a nose ring and harem pants until I met Flora. Let's give it a whirl.

I separated from her, glancing around furtively, unsure of what I was supposed to be doing. I thought, "Hey, pretty orange rock, are you calling to me? No? Okay. Have a nice day...."

I physically picked up a few crystals and examined them so the possibly-high sales girl would think I was at least trying (and maybe even a little clever and edgy, too).

It turns out that the rocks were actually really pretty if you paid attention. Shrugging a little to shake off my skepticism, I started to really *look* and *listen* for that call. It probably helped that I was still quite buzzed.

I don't know why I picked up the gorgeous blue stone with stripes running through it, except to say...I liked it. I put it in my hand. I felt its smooth, polished surface with my thumb. It was familiar. It felt heavy. It also, strangely, felt like it was already mine. I hadn't paid for it yet, but I just knew it was supposed to belong to me. How unexpected. Did this rock just *call* to me?

When I showed it to Flora at the checkout counter, her eyes narrowed as she grinned. "Ah, yes. Perfect." Then she giggled, and I reflexively giggled, too. I paid the yeah-I'm-sure-she's-very-high girl behind the counter 6 dollars.

We left, traipsing down the Chelsea street in our inadequate shoes—real New Yorkers never have real snow boots. Then, we both headed home on subway trains going in opposite directions, our pockets filled with our recent purchases.

*

I texted Flora a few days later: "What crystal did I buy?"

She replied, "I'm not going to tell you; that'll ruin it."

"Well, something happened—a good thing—I'm curious if it's just a coincidence or..." I typed.

"You finished writing your story, didn't you?"

I put the phone down for a long moment before replying: "Are you an actual, real-life witch? You can tell me."

I had mentioned to Flora, over my zinfandel and her merlot, that I had been experiencing writer's block. I'd been stuck on a short story I was writing for weeks, and I just couldn't figure out the ending. Then that very morning, I finished the story! I had placed my mystery crystal on my desk next to my computer, and—I couldn't explain it—I had the most successful day of writing I'd had in years. Why was that morning different?

I should mention at this point: I suffer from very common, very basic-B anxiety. Technically it's Generalized Anxiety Disorder; that's the diagnosis on the forms my therapist sends my insurance company. The severity had waxed and waned over the years. In the times it was bad, my anxiety stopped me from engaging in way too many things: parties, romantic relationships, friendships, and (most destructively) my own self-expression.

You know that feeling that you're faking every interaction you have with anyone, even yourself? I had that a lot.

I'd been in a pretty good place lately, except I still had my damned writer's block, which I knew was entirely because of my anxiety. If it wasn't perfect, why write the story at all, you know?

I'd tried all the usual stuff to clear my stress and anxiety up. Many conventional tactics worked at different times: exercise, visualization, breathing exercises, even drinking more water.

The results were always temporary. And now, a very unconventional method—crystals—worked practically overnight without me even realizing or planning it.

Maybe there is something to this, after all?

That day changed the course of my life. I started voraciously learning everything I could about crystals. My collection grew. My experiments with different practices became cherished rituals in my life. I had become… a crystal girl.

I have crystals all around my house. I have them in my pockets most days. I spend an embarrassing amount of time on Etsy looking for crystal jewelry. I'm in deep.

I also have read countless books and scholarly articles. I've watched 100s of hours of YouTube videos. I lurk on Reddit. I post in Facebook groups. I've been trying to learn ALL the secrets.

And I wrote this book to pass along everything I've collected on the subject, through research, through conversation, and (most importantly) through personal trial-and-error. You're going to read how practitioners have been using crystals for thousands of years and what modern folks are doing when they post Instagram pictures of crystals lined up on their bodies at expensive crystal healing retreats.

But, I'm also going to tell you what these crystals mean to me, an average girl, who can't pull off harem pants and a nose ring but is doing everything she can to manage her stress and anxiety, connect to her loved ones, be creative, and live the best life she can.

*

Up top, I feel I must acknowledge that the subject of crystals is a little woo-woo. To some, it has a bad reputation as pseudoscience or new-age nonsense. Skepticism is allowed and welcome! But I invite you to open your heart to the idea that some things are true, even if you can't put your finger on exactly why. The only way to know if it works is to try it with an open mind.

The scientific method, after all, suggests that trying something is the only way to know if it works! If the experiment fails, then all you've lost is a few dollars. Put the pretty rocks in a bowl in your bathroom, and call it a day. If the experiment *does* work... well, the benefits in your life can be enormous. So, what do you have to lose?

And let's talk about what I call the "spectrum of beliefs." Most people believe meditation works. Fewer people believe that crystals work. And fewer still believe that Wicca works. But they're all different points on the same line. They're all about spending focused time with your thoughts, your intentions, your breath, and your body. And, that kind of self-care is always worthwhile.

And one last thing before we jump in: Ultimately, crystals only work if you allow them to work. It takes a degree of faith, which is not a thing that comes easy to most of us in the 21st Century. But faith is easier if you have a friend to guide you. I had Flora. You have me. Let's go![1] [2]

1
WHAT ARE CRYSTALS, AND DO THEY ACTUALLY WORK?

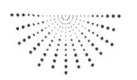

There's a piece of Quartz in my bra right now. No, really.

I'll admit, sometimes it's uncomfortable to keep a crystal there... but what if you don't have a pocket? What's a crystal girl to do? (Or crystal guy. I don't discriminate.) Yes, your bra is a convenient place to keep a crystal but also, putting a crystal in your bra means it's next to your heart. I've found that placement matters. So does skin contact. I recommend it (if you're a person that wears bras, of course). It works for me. But I'm getting ahead of myself.

This chapter will explore what crystals are, and how and why crystals work. This will set you up with the context to understand all the knowledge-bombs in the chapters to come. I'll also share a little bit more about my own experiences and practices to help you along. Most of my crystal practices are focused on my stress and anxiety, so if that's a problem we share... baby, we're going to go deep. But that's not all; some of my practices are much more straightforward.

For instance, one time, I put a piece of Clear Quartz in my bra (again) to help me fend off a cold. It boosted my strength and clarity by reminding me of my body's ability to handle anything that comes its way. It also was just kind of fun to have a secret rock in my bra, like my own private joke on the subway. When a creepy dude made eye contact, I stared him down until he looked away. I usually avoid *all* eye contact, but something about carrying a stone for courage made me feel courageous. I am woman, hear me roar (and possibly sneeze—I could definitely feel that cold coming on).

I don't just use my bra; that would be a little nutty. I use my pockets a lot.[1] I keep crystals all over my apartment. I also have a particularly flat crystal that I keep in my wallet. And, of course, *mounds* of crystal jewelry.

There are so many ways to make crystals work for you. I use them as desk ornaments, as home decor, as paperweights, as a focus when I meditate or do yoga, and a number of other ways.

For example, have you seen those trendy water bottles with the Rose Quartz inside? Rose Quartz vibrates with the energy of unconditional love, so it's an excellent crystal to motivate you for exercise and dieting. Drinking water that's been near a crystal lets that same unconditional love become part of you when you swallow it.

Who wouldn't want unconditional love in a bottle?

When you put it that way, it makes it sound like a love potion, but it's more about keeping your inner focus on loving yourself, just the way you are. I sometimes ruminate on how helpful a Rose Quartz necklace would have been for my dating life in high school, as a matter of fact. Enough said on that topic.

Let's start with the same question I asked when I walked into the crystal shop with Flora that day: "Aren't crystals just, well, rocks?"

On one level, that's true. They are rocks, of a kind. Did you know, though, that not all crystals are actually rocks? Some are fossils, some are minerals, some are true crystalline structures, and gemstones, too. In this book, I don't get very picky about the chemical makeup of each crystal. If you're a science-y type, by all means, look them up; the science you'll learn will be fascinating. For our purposes, I'm mostly concerned with their healing properties and the ways they've soothed my stress. And I'm hoping this book will help you quickly find the crystals you need, too.

Crystals are by no mean a modern fascination. The ancient Egyptians used to crush certain crystals up and use them as makeup, and of course, royalty has put precious gems in their crowns to show how fancy they are since ancient times. Warriors have put pretty stones on their armor for protection. Gems and stones have been used for centuries in all kinds of ways: as talismans, as part of ritual worship, as currency, and almost everything else you can think of.

There is something about these shiny rocks that keeps humans mesmerized.

Using crystals for healing purposes is part of a tradition that goes back to these early sages. If you think about it, though, coal, plastics, concrete, the inside parts of computers, and most other modern conveniences start out as minerals or rocks in some shape or form. So, we're not so different from the ancient mystics in the end. Still, we've begun to study and think about them in different ways over the centuries.

To explain the scientific properties of crystals, Flora, surprisingly, loves to quote Einstein, who said that everything is energy. (You'd think she'd be more likely to cite the Dalai Lama instead, wouldn't you?) When Einstein said everything is energy, he meant that everything vibrates. Rocks, chairs, oceans, stars, planets, sidewalks, computers, cell phones, fidget spinners, Xanax, merlots…everything.

At the atomic level, electrons are circling protons and neutrons at predictable intervals, creating a vibration with a predictable frequency. The vibration of a carbon atom, for instance, is always the same for every single carbon atom.

Minerals and crystals, like everything else, are made up of atoms bonded together. What makes crystals so perfect is that the atoms always line up in the exact same way. This creates the beautiful geometric shapes in Amethyst, for instance, and the uniform shine you see in a perfect Opal.

Let's look at Pyrite as an example, with the chemical formula FeS_2. That's one iron atom, with two sulfur atoms that always bond to each other in the same formation. Repeat that over and over, and you not only get a beautiful piece of Pyrite, but you get a piece of matter that is perfectly uniform. Each molecule vibrates at the same frequency, which means you can always count on a piece of Pyrite to vibrate at the same frequency—if you find it in a cave in Spain or in a piece of jewelry hanging from the neck of the guy who cuts your hair at the mall. Crystal frequencies are reliable in a way that most matter… just isn't.

You have a frequency, too. But sorry boo, you're not a crystal; you're all over the place.

You are changing at every moment, so the influence of a perfect, consistent vibration is sometimes exactly what you need. That's why crystals can "call" to us. Their frequency draws us to them by resonating with us in our own energetic vibration. They want to level you out, or to give you some new energy, or countless other things.

So, when I went into that shop for the first time, the Blue Lace Agate drew my attention because of the "everything is energy" thing. Its energy aligned with mine. Something in me said, "This rock is for me," and I bought it. Since then, I've used my own experience and research on crystals to build on what Flora showed me that first day.[2]

Healing crystals are special, as I said, since they're not structured like the average pebble you find in the park. But once you start learning to experience the frequencies of crystals, you can begin to experience the frequencies of all the things around you, and your mind really opens up to... well, everything. Now, I instinctively feel the energies of things I encounter, like random shells at the beach, my ceramic coffee mug, and even my houseplants. The frequencies of the plants in my apartment affect the frequency of my body. We're all connected. Everything is energy. It's humbling and inspiring to walk around the world like that.

And that all started for me with crystals, these

little pieces of perfection in design that feel like a gift from the planet. If you're a witch, you'd say they were a gift from Gaia, the Mother Earth goddess. For me, it's more about an amazing little bit of the divine that science has helped us uncover. It gives me goosebumps to think about.

So, Crystal girl/guy/non-binary individual, what do we do with this information? Well, we use what Gaia (or science) has generously given us. We use crystals to help align our frequencies to be whatever we want them to be. Just like when you take a pill or indulge in some wine, and the frequencies of those substances change your energy by merging with it, a crystal becomes a part of your energy system when you're near it.

Here's another helpful way to think about it: since energy radiates in all directions, you are actually *inside* your own energy field (rather than it being inside you). This is why crystals can benefit you even when they're in your pocket or sitting beside your bed. Their energy field merges with yours since energy fields are kind of like large bubbles surrounding each living thing.[3]

Okay, now that we've established what crystals are, let's talk about which ones might be right for you. All crystals, since they have their own unique, repeating, and finite molecular structure and corresponding energy frequencies, have their own properties and benefits. I'm sharing some of my favorites in this book, but there are literally thousands of options out there. The sheer variety of crystals can sometimes feel overwhelming, so hopefully, my experience will help you to find the crystals that are "calling" to you right now, just like that Blue Lace Agate called to me.

On some level, my "inner knowing" (more on that later) insisted that one *particular* shiny rock would be good for me. We were energetic matches, so to speak. Call me and the rock "cosmic soulmates," if you will.

So, why did the Blue Lace Agate make a difference in my writer's block? Agates are typically found in rivers and streams, so the flowing power of water is melded into their energy systems. Blue is a calming color that often helps people feel focused and relaxed. (Interior decorators use it in bedrooms and bathrooms. The color itself also has its own frequency.) When you put it all together, the Blue Lace Agate helps align my own frequency with calm and focus, just a little bit. Often, that's enough.

If you are an empathic or intuitive person, you will probably know right away what I'm talking about and be really good at knowing which crystals you need. If you don't have these abilities but want to develop them, all it takes is patience and practice.

CRYSTALS FOR THE MIND

You'll get there. After all, if someone like me can do it, you can too.

In a book called *The Crystal Bible,* Judy Hall writes that "crystals are powerful beings in their own right; they need to be approached with respect." In the same way, you can treat yourself as a powerful being deserving of respect while you take your crystal journey with me.

In *A Modern Guide to Crystal Healing*, Yulia Van Doren reminds us that we are all made of stardust. Indeed, you and me and the stars and the planets and everything else are made up of essentially the same building blocks: minerals created the moment the universe began.

When we recognize that, we remember that we are of infinite worth, literally made of the same stuff as stars. That's something I've had to wrestle with, but it's been ultimately so rewarding to recognize my own inner power. (As cheesy as it sounds, it works for me. Man, there are those goosebumps again!)

So, how do we use this revelation about our special place in the universe when we're sad or mad or just don't feel connected?

In the depths of my most anxious times, I think the *real* fear I face is, "what if I'm not good enough?" (Even though it disguises itself in so many ways, that's the crux of it all.) This is the reason I have a tendency to self-medicate: with alcohol, with drama, with Netflix, with using all my 10% off coupons from Bed, Bath and Beyond at once…you know, the usual stuff. Or rather, I *had* a tendency to self-medicate, before crystals came along.

Actually, at first, crystals were just another binge, until I realized that the real lesson here is that crystals don't "give" me good vibes. They bring out the good vibes that are already there.

The truth is that we are *all* good enough, and we are deserving of so much love and peace. That's what crystals teach us. If a small, ordinary-looking stone can say, confidently, "Hey, look at how cool I am," why can't we do the same?

Of course, we can't always own our own power, so it's nice when crystals can lend a helping hand. I've taken more than one prescription for anxiety, so I know what it feels like to suddenly have that undercurrent of panic taken away. When I bought the Blue Lace Agate and found that it helped my writer's block, it wasn't because I thought, "Wow, what a unique molecular structure! I'd like to get me some of that energy." I just thought it was pretty. And that Flora was edgy and that the very-very-high salesgirl would judge me if I didn't buy anything. I only noticed the benefits later on.

Just some of the benefits of crystals include better sleep, better mood, better appetite, weight loss, more energy, better relationships, better sex, self-care, and a whole host of other things too numerous to mention in just one book.

That's why healing crystals are so powerful and why professional crystal healers use them in healing sessions with clients one-on-one. They help clients find crystals that suit them and help them focus their attention for maximum benefit. They might place crystals on various parts of your body for specific ailments or help you set specific intentions for meditation.

However, you don't need a practitioner to use crystals! You can do it all on your own, with just a little guidance from books like this one.

For me, the Blue Lace Agate, somehow, helped me—like anxiety meds do, but in a more settled, steady way and for a specific purpose. It's almost as if the Agate found the focus already inside of me and brought it out, instead of creating the focus for me. And it lasted, even when I wasn't directly near the Agate. So, no need for a constant re-application, so to speak. (Unlike the lipgloss I bought at Bed, Bath and Beyond with those coupons. Um, why did I buy lipgloss at the same place I buy towels? I digress.)

✱

In a later chapter of this book, I will teach you

some practices and techniques to help you get the most out of your crystals. You can go full-hog-wild with crystal magic and incantations and the rest, or simply content yourself with crystal jewelry. The choice is up to you. There is no one right way to use crystals, although there are a few wrong ways.

A few ground rules just to get us started: If you read the part about drinking water with Rose Quartz in it and immediately put some in a glass, good for you! You're already enthusiastic, which means you and I will get along great. However, it's essential to not rush into things, like drinking crystal elixirs, without doing your homework first. Not all crystals are safe for drinking water, as some leach harmful toxins when wet. In general, keep most crystals away from water to avoid erosion over time. If you use crystals in drinking water, set aside specific, safe crystals that you will use to make your crystal elixirs. If you really, *really* want the properties of crystals in your drinking water but feel weird about drinking water with rocks in it, you can simply set your water bottle by the crystals overnight. Bottom line: make sure to research a crystal carefully before using it in water.

Most crystals are generally safe to use in your home or as jewelry though, as long as they come from a reputable source and don't seem damaged in any way. Read about each one and decide which ones are right for you to start out with, then build your collection over time. This book will give you plenty of basic details, but there are lots of resources out there you can turn to. Also, there will be a more detailed how-to guide later in this book to teach you how to care for your crystals in safe and responsible ways.

Lastly, and most importantly, make sure to have fun and do what feels good to you. Healing crystals are all about intuition and knowing what's best for your life at any given moment, so go with the flow and see what rocks can do for you!

*

This book will take you through my favorite crystals for dealing your mind—most specifically for managing stress and anxiety—including information, tips, and resources to help you utilize them to their full potential. I will also cover the ways crystals can assist with sleep, social situations, and other conditions related to mental stress but in more general terms. You can't get away from your brain, so it makes sense to have crystals that support a wide variety of mental benefits.

We all have our anxious moments, even if we don't classify ourselves as anxious people. Crystals can help, whether you're just going through a temporarily stressful time and need a little boost, or you've been anxious your whole life. Even if you're not an anxious person, you can still gain lots of benefits from these crystals (or you can use them to help a friend or loved one).[4]

Personally, I have been anxious since I was a kid, but didn't have an official diagnosis until much later. I honestly wish someone had taught me about energy and crystals at a much younger age so I wouldn't have had to go through so much trouble and strife. Now, though, I'm really grateful that I've had the chance to learn about things "the hard way," so to speak, so now I get the opportunity to talk about it with you.

Crystals make the hard parts of my life just a little easier by smoothing them out and helping me feel strong enough to deal with them. They take a lot of the hassle out of my daily life, and they've even helped me overcome much of my strife over time. My anxiety doesn't stress me out as much anymore, frankly. It's there, but it isn't debilitating like it used to be. I mean, I still have my moments…but they're not as earth-shattering as they once were.

In conclusion, I want to tell you that crystals have one more fantastic benefit. They can be powerful connection tools. I love noticing other people's crystals in public and striking up a conversation about them. It's incredible how often those conversations turn into deeper connections that last (like Flora and me). I'm excited to make this connection with you now, too.

> And don't forget to join my Facebook community, so we can all learn together. Post pictures of the crystals you find. Ask the crowd for suggestions. And meet some new crystal friends.
>
> www.facebook.com/groups/HealingCrystalsChangedMyDangLife

You ready? Good. Let's dive in!

2

CHOOSING YOUR CRYSTALS

Now that we've got some basics out of the way, let's focus on why you're reading this book: to learn how to overcome stress and anxiety with crystals. In the coming pages, we'll discuss choosing the right crystals for these specific needs.

But before we do this, now is the time for some self-examination. Let's think about what we actually want to accomplish. The critical question we need to examine is: **How do your feelings of stress and anxiety manifest themselves?**

So, simple, right? Not! Take a deep breath. This will take some personal work which can be very uncomfortable, but I'm here to help. And ultimately to offer some solutions![1] Let's get vulnerable like Brené Brown tells us we should be.

In that spirit, I'll start with myself as an example,

and maybe some of my thoughts will resonate with your experiences. I am generally stressed out and often anxious, yes, but how does that affect my day-to-day life? That's a complicated question, but I'm going to attempt to be really real with you here, readers.

- The first is a soft-ball: Immediately, I think that my anxiety really hinders my self-expression. I'm often too nervous to communicate well. This is bad news for a writer. Or a spouse. Or a mom. Or anyone, really.
- Here's something I never thought I'd admit in a book… My stress gives me major digestive issues. If I have an important meeting, you can be 100% sure I'm going to have a stomachache. Sometimes I will have cramps so bad I have to cancel that meeting. I genuinely worry about my long-term health if I don't master this issue.
- Stress also affects my overall wellness. When I'm extra anxious, it's harder to eat well, work out, sleep enough, shower, wear makeup, and all those other things I usually like to do to feel good. Then, when I don't feel thin enough or healthy

enough, the vicious cycle starts all over again.

- And, to be frank, when I'm anxious and someone I love doesn't behave exactly the way I want them to, I immediately assume they no longer like me. That's really hard to admit, but it's true. I know logically that the issue is in my head, but my immediate reaction is self-doubt. My anxiety makes it hard to love myself.
- Come to think of it, anxiety hinders me even when people behave the way I *do* want them to, as well. Here's an example: It's really hard for me to call people I don't know well. So, let's say I call a new friend and leave a voicemail asking if they'd like to have coffee. If this person calls me back, I'm 100% not answering that call. I mean, a call back is the reasonable expectation, but what if they're only calling back to let me down easy? Or, maybe they're pretending to be nice, and I'll only know if I dissect the person's tone in the voicemail. Or could they possibly, actually want to have coffee with me? Such pressure!

Does any of this sound familiar? I may sound like

a bit of a nut-job, but I bet you and I have some overlap. So, let's talk about it.

Now, *your* hard work begins: take the next few minutes to think about *your* stress and anxiety. What are some of the ways your anxiety is stopping you from living your best life? Does it encourage bad decisions? Does it sap your energy? Does it kill your sex life? Take a moment. I've provided some space below for you to write down your impressions. We'll use this later on in the book to choose crystals and to come up with some action steps we can take together to make some positive change.

ALLEGRA GRANT

1.

2.

3.

4.

5.

CRYSTALS FOR THE MIND

. . .

As we continue, keep these issues in mind. You're going to find not only crystals that match up to your concerns, but that these concerns are so common that generations and generations of healers have been working on soothing these issues. You're not alone. And I'm here to help.

I'm getting excited. How about you?

Later in the book, I'll tell you how I personally use crystals to help with my problems. If you're an absolute beginner, don't look up the crystals before you choose one. We've talked about this: find the ones you're drawn to, and experience what they do for you without prejudice.

In fact, I'm about to share with you my own process for choosing crystals. It's all based on something not many of us are taught these days: intuition.

Intuition is the "inner knowing" we get when we can't pinpoint the source of knowing something. We "just know" somewhere deep inside us. If you've ever been in a social situation that just felt "off" or avoided something on a hunch and then later found out you narrowly escaped disaster, this was your intuition giving you a clue. All humans have an inner compass that steers us from time to time.

After buying that first Agate, I wasn't sure where to go next. Flora, predictably, waved me off with a vague, "You'll know which ones are right for you," which felt like absolutely useless advice at the time.

I remember one time at Larissa's Christmas party —the first one I went to, actually, when I met Flora for the first time. We were standing in a group of people, clutching cocktail glasses and trying to seem witty and interesting. (Well, I was trying to seem witty and interesting. Everyone else was just... *doing* it, somehow. Am I the only one who goes all woozy in situations like that?)

Flora, predictably, was scintillating and funny, and I was trying to nod appreciatively at everything she said, even though I had often only a vague clue what she was talking about. Then, after a few minutes, she suggested that she and I go out on the balcony for some air. Naturally, I agreed. As soon as we were outside, she turned toward me, looked me in the eye, and said, "It's always nice to take a *moment,* isn't it?"

I had no idea how she knew that I was longing to step out on that balcony for some alone time, even if it was 30 degrees out. In fact, I'd been mentally planning how to slip away without seeming rude, carefully scoping it out, without making it obvious that I was planning an escape route. In my dazed, overawed state, I assumed she could read minds. I wouldn't have put it past her.

However, looking back, Flora is just really intuitive and empathic. She has the gift of seeing other people's needs and meeting them. It's like she feels *with* you. And she doesn't make it a whole thing, either. She just does it.

But here's the thing: it's not only Flora who can do this. We all can. We just don't always *know* that we can.

In the Western scientific world, we tend to favor data and evidence over intuition, which isn't right or wrong. It's just different. Intuition has its own biological basis, though. Scientists are beginning to explore more the biochemical factors involved in "inner knowing," which is innate to all species, including humans. Animals in the wild "just know" stuff because they are in tune with their physical bodies much more than we are. They can sense danger, migrate thousands of miles, avoid poisonous food, and all kinds of other incredible things because they really lean into the "inner knowing" found in the physical body.

Humans, though, have a tendency to be really in our heads. We love data and evidence; we are gifted with a powerful brain that can imagine and innovate and create…and also habitually overthink. As a classic over-thinker, my anxiety is often tied to weighing pros and cons, relying heavily on evidence, and over-analyzing every possible outcome in a given situation. Personally, I am always asking, "what if?"

Of course, there's nothing wrong with that, by itself. The human brain has brought about so many wonderful and exciting things in this world. I'm learning, though, that when I also think with my body (and not just my brain), I feel a lot more grounded and stable. By "trusting my gut," I have a lot more confidence in my decisions and spend much less time worrying over whether I've made the "right" decision or not. Sometimes something feels right in the moment, and that's good enough for now.

Crystals are the same way. When I entered the crystal shop for the first time, I was drawn to that first Blue Lace Agate because it felt nice in my hand, and I liked the color. I found out later that its unique frequency was calling to me because my body was saying I needed help with my writer's block.

Crystals are a great way to learn how to intuitively make decisions for yourself. You can pick a crystal because you *just know*. You can do this by choosing the crystals you're drawn to, or you can study the books, learn more about chakras, alignments, and frequencies to help you choose the crystals that match your particular energy needs.

As I got more in tune with crystals, I started to

notice that I could actually feel the energetic frequencies of each crystal when I held it in my hand. As soon as I picked one up, I could sense the power of the crystal, perhaps as a feeling in my heartspace or a tingling in my fingers. Sometimes it feels like a buzzing around my head or even a sensation of being rooted to the ground. Sometimes crystals incite a deep emotional detox for me, and I suddenly feel as if I'm about to cry. Sometimes I *do* cry, and just let it all out. It feels good. And then I usually laugh at myself for crying about a *rock*, of all things. That feels good, too.

If you're a naturally intuitive person, this all makes sense for you already. If you're not, that's okay. Over time, I have gotten more and more attuned to the frequencies of crystals. If you're saying to yourself right now that when you pick up a rock, it just feels like a rock, that's perfectly fine. You can literally just pick out some nice rocks for yourself and see what they do for your stress level. That's perfectly acceptable and equally as powerful.

Not everyone is sensitive to crystals in the same way, and I had to work very patiently with myself to understand and sense them, even though I found out I have some natural intuitive gifts to begin with. Some people experience crystals as a hot or cold feeling in the crystal itself. Some people suddenly remember things that happened in childhood or associate the crystal with an idea or belief they've had. It's different for everyone.

In the next chapter, I'll tell you about some of my favorite crystals, but for now, just go with the ones that you're naturally excited about or interested in. The rest of this chapter will provide a system for you to start tapping into your energetic needs and prepare you for learning more about specific crystals and how they can work for you.

Specifically, I'm going to teach you about how energy works in the human energy field so you can use the crystals for your own personal needs. Your energy field surrounds your whole body, as I mentioned in the previous chapter, and it also is *in* your body; it's like a large electromagnetic bubble that you are right in the middle of. Almost like a power grid in a large city, it's filled with criss-crossing lines, shapes, and energy spheres that correspond with different parts of your body and aspects of your life.

For the most part, your energy field takes care of itself. Your energy field is actually there to keep you flowing and balanced and has a tendency to "course correct" any time something gets out of whack.

When your energy field gets injured in some way (usually due to trauma, either mental, emotional, physical, spiritual, or some combination of the four), your body responds with a signal designed to alert

CRYSTALS FOR THE MIND

you to the problem. This signal might be an illness, a clumsy accident, an emotional outburst, fatigue, relationship troubles, or infinite other types of complications in your life.

From an energy perspective, all problems are imbalances in your energy field, and they are simply guideposts to teach you how to get back into balance. Since everything is energy, it doesn't matter if the problem is mental, emotional, physical, or spiritual. It all vibrates at a particular frequency, and energy ties these four dimensions together.

For me, my anxiety was one such problem. It was a signal from my energy field that said, essentially, "Hey! You've had too much trauma for too long!" I've been through some stuff in my life, some of it significant, some of it fairly minor, but it all adds up. Once I got into crystals and learned about energy, a practitioner taught me that my energy field had started to develop some holes and gaps, partly due to my innately anxious personality, partly due to genetics, and partly due to the baggage I carried with me from the stuff that had happened to me. The more stressed I got, the more these things started to add up, and the less my usual methods (pills, therapy, exercise, etc.) had any effect.

I breathed a huge sigh of relief when I learned that I wasn't broken, just traumatized (more on that later). Most of us are at least slightly traumatized by the regular bumps and bruises of living on this planet. Many of us are *very* traumatized. It's a lot to carry in any case.

Later into my journey with crystals, Flora shared with me that she had a *very* traumatic childhood. And young adulthood. After working with her traumas through energy and crystal healing, they got better.[2]

That's the good news: using energy and crystals means you can approach physical problems from a mental perspective…or mental problems from an emotional perspective…or emotional problems from a spiritual perspective…you get the idea. If your mental solutions to your mental problems aren't really working, try attacking them from a different angle. (Or physical solutions to physical problems, whatever. It all connects, in the end). Since anxiety presents itself as a mental problem, I started using physical and spiritual interventions (crystals) to see the problem from a different perspective.

And hey, what can I say? – it really helped.

*

There are dozens of energy perspectives out there, but the one that has resonated the most with me is the chakra system. Chakras, or "wheels" in Sanskrit, are energy centers in the human energy field. By understanding our chakras, we can note places that need a little balancing and choose crystals that assist with the process.

Specifically, crystals for chakras are often grouped by color, as they correspond to the colors generally associated with each specific chakra. Acupuncture, massage, Reiki, meditation, and many other healing modalities utilize the chakras to understand and release energy imbalances in the human energy system.[3]

To start, you need to know how many chakras there are and what they represent before you can really tap into them! There are seven main chakras in this system, although your body has literally thousands of chakras. It's easiest to just stick with seven, at least for our purposes. I'll describe each of them here, so you can get a (very brief) idea of what they're like.

The chakra system is organized around a color system, a guideline adapted from ancient Eastern thinkers. People sometimes argue that the chakra colors are highly arbitrary and invented by modern Western practitioners more recently. That may actually be the case, but that's okay with me. Using the chakra colors helps me keep everything organized and neat in my head (and in my house). And the vibrations of each color go really well with the purposes of their matching chakras, which I don't think is an accident. And obviously, color is a major reason we love to look at crystals, since they're so fascinating.

By learning a little bit about each chakra, you can start to notice where you might have imbalances in your life and can start to work on them with the right crystals. Personally, I found out that *most* of my chakras needed a boost, most of the time, and that's perfectly okay, too. Finding balance within yourself can be really rewarding, and even fun, at times. Of course, be gentle with yourself when working with chakras, because traumas can come up. Doing more research about each chakra will probably help you, so check the resources at the end of this book for more information. In the meantime, here's a *brief* (and I mean very brief) overview of each chakra, focusing on how that chakra can contribute to your anxiety and stress level if it's out of balance. Plus, I'll list some crystals related to each chakra.

The first chakra is the **root chakra**, which resonates with the frequency of Planet Earth. Located near the base of your spine, the root chakra reminds us to stay grounded and centered, like a tree with deep roots. Red, black, and brown are typical root chakra colors for crystals, including Red Jasper, Black Tourmaline, and other deep-earth stones.

For me, the root chakra is possibly the most important chakra for dealing with anxiety. I work

CRYSTALS FOR THE MIND

on it constantly to try and stay grounded. When I'm not grounded, I feel spacey, out of touch, constantly worried, and stuck on details that I later find out don't matter (you know, the kind that are instantly resolved when you eat a snack or take a nap). Root chakra crystals are excellent for sleep, stability, and security.

Located right beneath your belly button, the **sacral chakra** governs some vital internal organs nearby, along with creativity, productivity, and sexuality. The sacral chakra resonates with the color orange and teaches us that we are playful, powerful beings who make our own choices for the sheer joy of living. The sacral chakra teaches me to let loose and just enjoy life—which I cannot do when I'm wallowing in stress.

If my sacral chakra is out of balance (it usually is), I feel like I'm on an emotional roller coaster, my needs never seem to be met, and my relationships have all kinds of drama. If you've ever gone to a yoga class and had an emotional moment in pigeon pose, that's your sacral chakra releasing some crud as you open up your hips.

Sacral chakra crystals are great for letting your hair down and just feeling free—Carnelian and Citrine are great examples. They're also really positive, bright colors for rocks. It always surprises me to see an orange crystal like Citrine or Carnelian, but in a good way, you know?

Your **solar plexus** chakra is a bright yellow chakra right beneath your ribcage, another hot spot for internal organs. The solar plexus teaches us to honor our personal power—I can't think of anything more disempowering than anxiety. When my solar plexus chakra is out of whack (usually harboring old anger that I need to cleanse), I am anxiously attached, more co-dependent, and overly focused on controlling outcomes. It can also make me prone to angry outbursts because I've "swallowed" my emotions instead of honoring and accepting them in healthy ways.

As I mentioned, anxiety and stress often manifest for me as stomach issues due to stuff in my life I feel I can't "digest" in some way. When I'm overwhelmed, it's usually because my solar plexus needs a little love. Solar plexus crystals support confidence, self-respect, and healthy boundaries. They're typically golden, yellow, or amber-colored and support optimism and empowerment to move forward in life. Tiger's Eye and Pyrite are some of the most common.

The **heart chakra** is located (surprise!) in your heartspace, right in the center of your chest. It uses green and pink as its colors and represents uncondi-

CRYSTALS FOR THE MIND

tional love, acceptance, and growth. Rose Quartz and Malachite are two of my favorites.

When my heart chakra is closed, I feel closed off, disconnected, and generally angry at the world. Of course, chakras close up due to trauma, and heart chakras are particularly susceptible. If you've been hurt, your heart chakra will naturally close off a little, and that's okay. It's healthy, in fact. Supporting your heart chakra in gently opening back up again can be so powerful.[4]

Heart chakra stones are calming, warming, and energizing. They support transformation and trauma release. An open heart is a happy heart; since love is the opposite of fear, heart chakra crystals support you in loving yourself unconditionally. When I'm super anxious, I assume I'm worthless, and no one likes me, toss me a heart chakra stone and give me a few minutes alone. I'll be fine in no time.

If chakras can be too closed, they can also be too open—the **throat chakra** is an excellent example of this (although it's true of every chakra on this list). Located at your throat (bet you weren't expecting that, huh?), the throat chakra governs communication and living your truth, including knowing when to speak and when to listen. Throat chakra crystals are blue, usually lighter electric blues or pastels. An overactive throat chakra leads me to try too hard to prove I'm cool (you know, like that time I bought the Blue Lace Agate just to show off? Yeah, just like that).

An underactive throat chakra leaves me "holding my tongue," so to speak, and afraid to speak up for my needs, my beliefs, and my truths. It's *definitely* tied to my social anxiety and flips back and forth between closed and overactive all the time. When it's balanced, though, I can speak and write clearly and feel confident in being myself without having to *prove* I'm myself, if that makes any sense. Amazonite is another excellent example.[5]

Just like your other chakras, your **third eye chakra** can be overactive and encourage overthinking. It can be underactive and encourage close-mindedness (which is really just the fear of the unknown, after all). Both are stress- and anxiety-inducing for me. Your third eye is located on your forehead, just above the center of your eyebrows. Its colors are deep indigo blue and purple, and third eye stones encourage intuition, insight, and spiritual gifts.

When my third eye chakra is overactive, I have lots of vivid dreams and nightmares, which is obviously not fun. I also tend to second-guess my intuition, overthink it, and then slightly hate myself for being the way I am. Lots of trauma can get stored in the third eye if you haven't been able to develop your intuition, so it's essential to keep this clear. Third eye stones support good sleep, restful thinking, relaxation, and a calm outlook on life. I love Amethyst and Lepidolite for the third eye.

Last but certainly not least, the **crown chakra** rests just above the top of your head, and it represents your connection to everything. No, really, I mean *everything*. Since everything is energy, your crown chakra represents the harmony between literally everything that is, was, or ever will be.

As the root chakra connects you to the earth, the crown chakra connects you to the heavens and everything in it (remember, you are made of stardust). It teaches us that we are all One, in the end. When I'm highly anxious, I feel totally alone: I feel like no one knows me, understands me, or even likes me, frankly. It's sometimes a bit like feeling invisible, which is terrifying. The crown chakra reminds us that we are never alone, that we are always part of something bigger than ourselves. That's why crown chakra stones are so filled with serenity and peace. They are usually white, purple, or translucent, sometimes iridescent or with a pearly sheen. Selenite is one of my absolute favorite crystals of all time, and it's a powerful crown chakra stone.

✱

Overall, all of the chakras can be really useful for

a perspective into particular aspects of your anxiety and stress. Maybe they even resonate with some of the items you listed at the beginning of this chapter. Now that you've read a little about the chakras, take some time here to note which ones resonate with you the most. If there are any that jump out at you right off that bat, that's a great place to start. However, sometimes if I have a hard time articulating what a chakra means, it's because that chakra needs a bit of work. It's different for everyone, so you will need to spend some time getting to know yourself and your needs.

Actually, let's do a brief chakra exercise right here and now. It'll help you develop your intuition and prepare you for the next chapter when we finally begin to talk about individual crystals. As you do this exercise, make sure to be gentle with yourself and go slowly. Sometimes we bury intense emotions so far down that we don't even know they're there; sometimes, these emotions lie just beneath the surface, desperate for release. Be mindful of your needs and allow yourself to feel anything you need to feel at your own pace.

Alright, here's the chakra exercise. Start by breathing slowly into your first chakra (the root chakra, remember—located at the base of your spine). Focus your attention on it, and see it as a bright, glowing orb of crimson light. What is coming up for you? Are there any emotions, memories, or sensations that accompany it? If you don't notice anything right now, that is okay. Just make a note of it, and move on. As you practice, you'll get better at it. Take as long as you need, even days or weeks of focusing on the root chakra to see what you can learn.

Here's some space to jot down anything that might have shown up in your root chakra:

Next, focus on your sacral chakra, just below your belly button. Breathe slowly into it, and notice anything that comes up. Jot it down:

Now, tune into your solar plexus chakra, right beneath your ribcage. Breathe slowly into this area and notice anything that comes up. Make a note of anything that shows up for you:

. . .

Next, try your heart chakra. You might find it's easy to tap into. Breathe into your heartspace, not forgetting the backside of it, right beneath your shoulders. What is coming up for you? Make a note of it here:

The throat chakra comes next. Breathe into it, noticing how it connects with your mouth and nose, as well as your shoulders. Make a note of any sensations or emotions:

Now, breathe into your third eye chakra, just above the center of your eyebrows. What is coming up for you? Make a note:

. . .

CRYSTALS FOR THE MIND

Lastly, focus on your crown chakra, right above the top of your head. Breathe into it, and make a note of what comes to mind. Jot it down here:

To finish the exercise, spend a few moments breathing gently into anywhere else that might need some attention, making a note of wherever it might be located. It might be between chakras or in a specific internal organ. There's no wrong way to feel right now. Just honor the process and trust your intuition—it knows more than your mind. Make a note of anything else here:

Which chakras had the most "baggage" in them? Those are the chakras that might benefit from a crystal or two. Look for crystals in those colors and start to play around with crystals that seem to speak to your needs. We'll talk more about how to use crystals for healing specific chakras in a later chapter, but for now, just start finding crystals and seeing how you feel called to use them. Remember, there's no real wrong way to use crystals, as long as you use common sense.

Alright, hopefully, by now, you can see why chakras can be such a helpful way to view anxiety and why crystals can be so supportive to you in overcoming it. When I started to do this work, I discovered all kinds of things about myself that I had no clue I didn't know then; it's becoming a life-long quest, and I love it.

Keep this self-assessment in mind, as well as the worksheet of the ways your anxiety and stress show up in your life from the previous chapter as we go forward. This is the raw material that will help you find the perfect crystals for you. You're about to make some amazing discoveries in the next chapter as we go through specific crystals and stones and discuss what they're usually used for. This part is fun!

3

27 CRYSTALS FOR ANXIETY AND STRESS

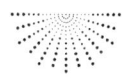

Remember, I began this journey on a whim. I wasn't even sure what needed healing in my life. As I learned more about crystals, I noticed that the crystals I was drawn to all had similar properties, which made me realize that they were all attempts to overcome stress caused by anxiety. It's almost like my anxiety was coming up for healing, soaking up all the good vibes the universe had to offer. Bring it on, I said to myself. Let's get this under control.

I hope the previous chapters inspired you to go and get some crystals of your own, using your own inner guidance. However, now I'm going to list some of my favorite crystals for anxiety and stress, just to get you started if you're still needing some more specific inspiration. Get your pen ready to start circling your top choices!

In this chapter, I organized the crystal suggestions by chakra to go along with the techniques and tips from the previous chapter, but you can peruse them in any order. Move to the ones that "speak" to you and come back to the ones that don't later (or never).

Keep in mind that the chakra groupings I use here are mere guidelines—other crystal practitioners might group them differently than I did. They're organized by color this way, too, to go along with each chakra. I also included small suggestions for using these crystals in the brief explanations. There will be more ways to use crystals to their highest potential in the next chapter, and these suggestions will connect with those.

CRYSTALS FOR THE MIND

Without further ado, may I present twenty-seven crystals that can help soothe anxiety and stress.

There is a gallery of full-color photos on my website, if you'd care to take a closer look.

Go to: www.allegragrant.com/27crystals

Or scan this QR code to be taken directly to the gallery:

ROOT CHAKRA CRYSTALS

As I mentioned, your root chakra "grounds" you, a crucial mechanism for feeling stable. Root chakra stones help with anxiety and stress because they help you feel rooted in the security of your own center, harder to pull off balance.

Black Tourmaline

A highly grounding stone, Black Tourmaline resonates with the frequency of Mother Earth. Black Tourmaline makes us feel safe, connected, and deeply "rooted," like a mighty oak no storm could blow over. Naturally, this stone is good for the root chakra, the chakra that connects you to the earth. Carry this stone in a pocket or wear it on a bracelet, or place it near your feet while you sleep. Tourmaline comes in a variety of colors, so see which one works for you, but Black Tourmaline is especially good to have with you when "earthing," the practice of walking barefoot on the earth for stress relief. You can also sit or lie on the ground to get a similar effect.

Lava Stone

A highly porous and surprisingly light stone, Lava Stone is another grounding stone. Because it's literally made of hardened lava, Lava Stone resonates with the deepest-of-deep earth energies, along with the cleansing, protective energy of the fire element. In other words, it's good for your root chakra because it comes straight from the earth—it literally bursts out of the ground in fountains, only to be hardened instantaneously.

Its porous nature also makes it really handy for aromatherapy. Take a drop or two of your favorite essential oil (and there are dozens of calming ones perfect for stress relief) and place it on your Lava Stone. The essential oils will gently diffuse throughout the day, dispersing softly into the air from the stones. Try purchasing a Lava Stone bracelet or necklace and dropping some oil right onto it; you will carry the energy of the stones (with the added bonus of aromatherapy) with you all day. My favorite essential oils for stress relief include lavender, valerian, copaiba, and vetiver, although there are dozens of great options. The oils will absorb straight into the stones and then dissipate without leaving much of a residue, although you are welcome to gently rinse your Lava Stones from time to time if there is too much oil built up. Rinsing in water will eventually dissolve the stones, though, so only do this occasionally.

Hematite

Another very grounding stone, Hematite is a dark gray stone similar to lodestone (the dark gray magnetic stones often found in gift shops—one of the many reasons men, women, and children of all ages love this particular crystal). A robust, shiny stone, Hematite helps you feel connected to the earth when you have a tendency to feel scattered or "up in the clouds." It's also a highly protective stone, good for dispelling negative energies. So if people around you are "in your space," so to speak, try Hematite. Personally, there is nothing more stress-inducing to me than having people disrespect my personal boundaries. Hematite is a good reminder that, no matter what happens, I am safe.

Red Jasper

I have already mentioned Red Jasper's ability to help you feel strong and courageous, an especially valuable quality when dealing with anxiety. Red Jasper emanates the energies of stability and strength and resonates with the frequency of the root chakra. It can help with emotional balance, trust, and security, as well as anything that requires additional moxie. Red Jasper was used historically to adorn armor and weapons, so keeping one (or two or three) in your pocket can let out your inner warrior god/goddess when you need them. It also supports energy flow (*chi*), so when I'm feeling depleted after an anxiety-ridden day, it can be a helpful stone to get me through the evening. Better yet, grab it in the morning when you feel stressed about what you have to face that day.

Smoky Quartz

Smoky Quartz is known for its ability to calm a panic attack right down. Its translucent, smoky surface connects the crown and root chakras, bringing you almost instantly into alignment. It's also a highly protective stone, so it can ward off bad juju—it's another one that was used to decorate weapons, and the ancient Druids used it frequently in rituals. I actually use this one with our dog. He gets anxious when we leave him home alone for too long, so I keep a chunk or two near his bed and food bowl area (although I set it up high so he can't get to it and hurt himself somehow... he's clumsy).

SACRAL CHAKRA CRYSTALS

Many of us develop anxiety in the years when our sacral chakra develops (3-7 years), so it's beneficial to clear out any traumas that you might still be holding there. Reframing with crystals can be a powerful cleansing tool for excess fears and worries in your life.

Carnelian

A red-to-orange stone, Carnelian resonates with the sacral and root chakras, meaning it's good for connecting to your inner Earth goddess. An excellent stone for boosting fertility and sexuality on the physical level, it's also excellent on the mental and emotional levels as it promotes creativity, productivity, and stamina to carry out your hobbies and creative ventures. An uplifting, energizing stone,

Carnelian invites you to take action, filling you with confidence and courage. Try using this stone while attempting a new craft or project you might have always wanted to try but never had the energy for. Even if you're "not good at art," try painting or dancing or writing poetry or something you've never done, just to see if you can, and take Carnelian along with you. You might be surprised at how good it feels!

Moonstone

Moonstones are famous throughout history as precious gems and come in various colors (cream, peach, white, etc.). Moonstone is a calming, balancing stone that invites harmony and serenity, especially during—*ahem*—that time of the month. Resonating with the clarity and sensitivity of the moon, moonstone awakens feminine energies and can help balance yin and yang in your life. If you are feeling pulled off-center in the hustle and bustle of daily living (a very yang/masculine energy for many people), the feminine wisdom of the moonstone can fill you with inner peace and quiet. A shimmery, iridescent stone, moonstones make gorgeous jewelry. Since change can be scary and unsettling, it's helpful to have a moonstone around to remind you that all of life has its ups and downs—you can stay centered even when things around you feel off-balance.

Kyanite

Kyanite is a workhorse for stress and anxiety relief, as it clears blockages and attunes your spiritual gifts. Kyanite actually comes in a variety of colors, each corresponding to different chakras, so figure out which colors you are drawn to. In fact, this is true of many crystals (such as Tourmaline), so always keep this guideline in mind moving forward. Orange Kyanite is excellent for the sacral chakra, while Green Kyanite is good for the heart chakra; Blue Kyanite is a powerful throat chakra stone. Black Kyanite grounds you through the root chakra. Whichever variety of Kyanite works best for you, it's a calming, relaxing stone that never needs cleansing or charging, as it's a powerful cleanser in and of itself. Overall, Kyanite helps your chakras come into alignment, balances yin and yang energies, and works with the spiritual body as well as the physical body.

SOLAR PLEXUS CHAKRA CRYSTALS

Like I said in the last chapter, your solar plexus radiates with your own personal power. I can't think of anything more *dis*empowering than my anxiety (which affects so many areas of my life), so boosting my power is my main goal with these crystals.

Citrine

A highly cleansing crystal, Citrine is one of the few stones that will seldom need to be cleansed. In fact, it can cleanse other stones if you place them with enough Citrine. Citrine resonates with the solar plexus chakra and is known as the crystal of luck and prosperity, which means that Citrine helps with money woes. Money can be a stress-inducing topic, so use this one when thinking about business ventures or doing your taxes (an event that drove me to self-medication every single time—until I started using Citrine). Citrine helps with confidence and success, so it's a go-to crystal whenever I have something important coming up at work! A good affirmation for Citrine is, "I stand in my power."

Pyrite

Although it's also known as "fool's gold," Pyrite is not for foolish people. It's for anxious people. Stemming from the Greek word for "fire," Pyrite is an energizing, confidence-boosting, protective stone that can light a "fire" within you by giving you strength to tackle whatever comes your way. It also sparkles very much like gold, so it always makes me feel powerful just by looking at it. It's an excellent stone for abundance if money is one of the things that keeps you up at night. Pyrite resonates with the solar plexus chakra and holds up a "mirror" to the self, allowing your true nature to come out and play (even if it sometimes gets hidden behind a wall of anxiety).

Tiger's Eye

A powerful protection stone, Tiger's Eye is named after, well, the eye of a tiger. Tiger's Eye resonates with the solar plexus chakra, reminding you to own your personal power. If you need to deal with narcissists, sociopaths, or just plain difficult people, the Tiger's Eye can be a powerful boost of self-confidence and inner fire. Anxiety tends to make me believe that I'm small and insignificant, so I use this one for performances and presentations (or any time I need to let out a ferocious inner tiger that can tackle any obstacles in her path). It works especially well on a long necklace that hangs down by the solar plexus chakra (and looks exceptionally witchy dangling there, too).

Amber

Amber is fossilized tree resin. It's an excellent physical pain reliever, but it's also a fantastic emotional pain reliever. You might have seen babies wearing it around their necks for teething pain. A comforting, relieving crystal, Amber can reduce common stress symptoms, specifically fatigue, exhaustion, as well as headaches (a major one for me). Really, it's just like Tylenol, except you don't have to swallow it. Amber comes in a variety of lovely necklaces and bracelets and is a widely available option.

HEART CHAKRA CRYSTALS

Since the heart chakra regulates emotions and connection, it's a crucial chakra for soothing anxiety. These crystals will help open the heart to unconditional love—which is the opposite of stress, fear, and doubt.

Rose Quartz

Rose Quartz is the ultimate heart chakra stone. The heart chakra colors are green and pink, so this one takes care of the pink side of that spectrum. It also radiates with unconditional love, both for self and others. All too often, anxiety includes self-hatred—we worry we're not good enough, we're afraid we're going to mess up, we're positive that nobody likes us. Rose Quartz reminds us that we are perfect, just the way we are. Having a little reminder of unconditional love to go with us throughout our day can be powerful. I love to wear this one as a necklace, sometimes even inside my clothing, right next to my heart. It serves as a reminder in meetings, out in public, while exercising, and any other time: that the extent to which I can offer love to myself is the extent to which I will receive it from others.

Malachite

Malachite is a really popular stone for stress and anxiety relief, as it's perfect for emotional detox and trauma release. By connecting you with the deep green energies of the heart chakra, Malachite connects you with the energy of growth. Uplifting, harmonizing, and supportive, Malachite seems to whisper, "everything is gonna be okay!" Helpful to wear to therapy or while meditating, it's a stone of transformation, helping you let go of post-traumatic stress, memories of abuse, or other heavy things you no longer want to carry in your energy field.

Ironically, it's a detox stone with toxic properties. It's one of those stones you should *never* use to make a crystal elixir, although it's totally safe to wear as jewelry. If you have experienced trauma, be gentle with yourself when allowing old emotions to come up. Malachite can support this process, just be mindful not to overdo it and always be kind to yourself, remembering that trauma is never the fault of the traumatized person.[1]

Bloodstone

Bloodstone is often considered a root chakra stone, but I'm putting it here for a few reasons. For one thing, it connects the root chakra with the heart chakra. For another, it governs circulatory issues (which is why it's a "blood" stone—it deals with anything to do with blood, which runs through… you guessed it…the heart). Also, it's mostly a deep green with flecks of red. Because Bloodstone aligns your upper and lower chakras, it's conducive to finding balance. Your lower chakras ground you to your physical self. Your heart serves as a "bridge" between body and mind, and we want that bridge to be healthy and strong. Anxiety tends to keep us out of our bodies and in our minds, so by connecting the heart with the root, Bloodstone re-routes that process by keeping us planted firmly. Bloodstone speaks of courage and strength in the face of adversity, a beneficial tool when dealing with stressful scenarios that come up.

Emerald

You're probably already familiar with emeralds as a gemstone, but did you know they are healing stones, too? You can use the fancy-cut emeralds that you find in jewelry, or you can purchase raw, uncut emeralds. Both are wonderful. For deep emotional healing, though, raw emeralds are my go-to choice. Emeralds support transition and growth and a balance between emotional and physical health. They can tap into and release the deep psychological causes of physical illness (and vice versa). This is a powerful one for me; be gentle with yourself when you use Emeralds!

THROAT CHAKRA CRYSTALS

As a person with high social anxiety, I need a clear throat chakra! These throat chakra stones assist with clear communication and openness, which is really helpful when navigating stressy social situations.

Blue Lace Agate

As I mentioned already, Blue Lace Agate is an excellent stone for communication. Living your truth means being your honest, balanced self—not too open, not too secretive. This can be a tricky balance to find! Blue Lace Agate is your partner in crime the next time you need to say something bold or put yourself out there. If you are a writer, speaker, singer, actor, journalist, teacher, influencer, academic, or any other form of communication worker, this stone will assist you in expressing yourself clearly and with confidence.

Of course, there's nothing more nerve-wracking than the fear of expressing yourself, so keeping one in your pocket or wearing it as jewelry can be profoundly comforting for stress-inducing communication scenarios. That can be things like breaking up with someone, asking for a raise, quitting your job, setting boundaries with someone, or any other "hard conversations" you need to have. It can also assist with releasing judgment (of yourself or others) for a more balanced approach to life.

Amazonite

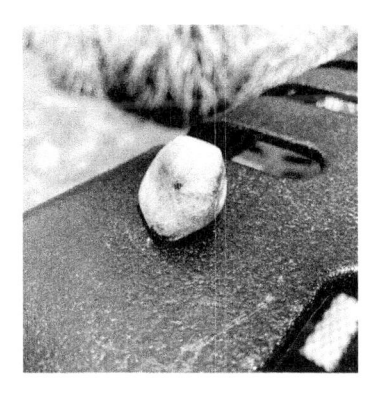

Another excellent stone for communication, Amazonite is sometimes called the stone of hope. It can help you speak your wishes into reality, and it can also be really supportive when you need to state your case or make an argument. Amazonite is a courageous, uplifting stone that can help with creativity and positivity. It makes beautiful jewelry and is a highly calming and protective stone, soothing to the brain and nervous system. This would be an excellent stone to place near you while you sleep if you want beautiful dreams about what is possible for your life. Or, as a kind gesture, place some under your partner's side of the bed to give them beautiful dreams too.

Chrysocolla

Chrysocolla helps us know when to speak, and when to shut up—possibly our most powerful communication skill. It brings out our inner wisdom, promoting peace through its gentle, soothing energy that encourages expressing our deepest feelings with dignity and strength. It's bright blue and gold; a beautiful stone that allows our experiences to teach ourselves (and to teach others). Since our experiences are our most influential teachers, being able to express them is critical when working through anxious thoughts. Personally, being able to talk through my past with friends and therapists has been one of my most powerful tools for dealing with anxious thoughts. Chrysocolla can support that process. If I were a therapist, I'd put a big chunk of Chrysocolla right next to the the chair the clients sit in.

Aquamarine

Resonating with the gentle, soothing power of the ocean, Aquamarine reminds me of the calm just beneath the surface of the water. Sometimes called "the stone of courage," Aquamarine is calming for social anxiety and nurturing for your personal truths. By helping us let go of control, Aquamarine reminds us that change is inevitable and will be okay (just like the waves flowing in and out from the shore). It helps quell angry, jealous thoughts and is one of my all-around favorites. Aquamarine makes beautiful bracelets; it's definitely something a mermaid would wear—just saying.

THIRD EYE CHAKRA CRYSTALS

Your third eye is located in your brain, often (but not always) the seat of anxious thoughts. Sometimes an overactive third eye is even the *cause* of anxious thoughts. So, calming the third eye can be a really powerful tool. Give some of these third eye crystals a try.

Amethyst

If you're looking for a good stone for the third eye *and* unconditional love, look no further. Love is the opposite of fear, so holding an amethyst immediately brings me back from the edge. More importantly, though, a lot of fear tends to hang out in our third eye chakra, right in our foreheads (not coincidentally, near our brains). Amethyst has been used for centuries to prevent drunkenness—the jury is

CRYSTALS FOR THE MIND

still out on whether that really works or not—but it also works well to invite good dreams and ward off negativity. To me, Amethyst speaks of connecting the head and heart—it gets me "out of my head" (away from overthinking) and into a more heart-centered approach to life. Wearing Amethyst earrings is an excellent way to keep them close to the third eye. It's also a good stone to have near you while you sleep. An Amethyst nightlight would be a perfect gift for a new baby.

Violet Fluorite

Although Fluorite comes in a variety of colors, Violet Fluorite (also called Purple Fluorite) is an excellent stone for the third eye chakra. Its primary vibration is that of peace. It supports mental acuity and speed, which is so helpful to me when my brain feels "bogged down" by all the tension that rattles around inside it. Violet Fluorite is particularly helpful for brain fog, confusion, conflicting ideas, or any other mental turmoil you might experience. It's also really handy for mental focus. An excellent stone for intuition, it can help you develop your "inner knowing" and bring it to new heights.

Lepidolite

Lepidolite is good for both the third eye and crown chakras, and it's great for calm and balance. It connects us with the angelic realms for maximum tranquility and serenity. It can be really powerful for a restful, calming sleep. As a powerful talisman against overthinking, Lepidolite seems to take a deep, cleansing breath for us, welcoming in gentle transition by releasing old psychological patterns. Its mottled purple and white (or soft pink and white) surface reminds me of the deepest galaxies in space, almost like floating in a perfect void, with no worries or cares. Looking at Lepidolite while you meditate will remind you of your place in the universe, which is both humbling and empowering.

CROWN CHAKRA CRYSTALS

The crown chakra connects us to All That Is. As Flora would say, connection to the Universe means we never have to live in fear. Disconnection is stress-inducing for *very* good reasons. In fact, most of my anxiety comes from disconnection: disconnection from my goals, from my dreams, from my spouse, from my family, from the people on the street. These stones remind us that, in the end, we are more alike than we are different.

Clear Quartz

Although Quartz comes in many varieties, Clear Quartz is known as a workhorse crystal. A highly versatile stone, Clear Quartz does so many great things for the body, mind, and spirit (such as fending off colds and assisting with courage on the subway, as you already know). Often called "the master healer," Clear Quartz carries a calming energy that promotes mental clarity and peace, along with improving memory and soothing irrational fears. As an amplifier, it will boost positive thoughts while it clears out negative ones. It also works really well in conjunction with other crystals, which we'll talk more about soon.

Lithium Quartz

This photo is by Yvette Kojic

Technically speaking, Lithium Quartz works with *all* the chakras, but my personal opinion is that its *real* focus is the crown chakra, which has a tendency to resonate with the frequencies of every chakra, all at once. So, Lithium Quartz can provide clarity and peace in *every* chakra, especially the crown chakra, where we often carry so much of our stress. Lithium Quartz is a gentle, pleasing stone that is honestly just really, really nice to look at. It sort of feels like gazing into the depths of the cosmic void. It also leaves you with a sweet sense of inner joy. Lithium Quartz varies from a soft pink to a pale purple or mauve color, with gentle variations deep in its translucent surface. This one can gently move old emotions to the surface to be healed, so be kind to yourself when working with this one. If you're needing some extra support detoxing emotionally from an intense therapy session (which I know I often do), Lithium Quartz might be just the ticket. (This is one of those crystals that you should *never* place in water—always do your homework when using crystals you're unsure of!)

Howlite

Howlite is a white and gray (almost like marble) calming stone that is excellent for sleep. If you've ever experienced anxiety-induced nightmares or "stress dreams," give Howlite a try. Its energy is that of serenity and peace, and it can invite in good vibes and dispel negative ones. You might create your own handmade dream-catcher and weave Howlite beads into the strings. (There are instructions on how to do this online.) Howlite is often paired with Lava Stones on bracelets, a perfect combination for cleansing your aura and keeping you grounded. Howlite is also an excellent abundance stone for when you're worried about money. A good affirmation to use with Howlite is: "Everything happens at the right time and for the right reasons."

Selenite

Possibly my favorite crystal of all time, Selenite resonates with the crown chakra and the frequency of the moon. Selenite is a cleansing, protective stone that repels negative energies and clears any residual angst in your energy field. Since Selenite cleanses the aura, it's excellent for removing other people's "junk" that they might have deposited on you during the day. When I hold it, it feels like a vortex to the universe opens through the crown of my head. Selenite is also the absolute best stone for cleansing your other crystals. Not only does it not absorb negative energies, but it also emits a strong cleansing frequency that washes away anything that does not serve your highest and best good. I keep a large chunk of Selenite on my nightstand (it's the kind that comes with a light so I can use it as a lamp) and a smaller chunk on my desk for clarity while writing.[2]

*

So, there you have it! Like I said before, make sure you don't take my word for it. Experiment! These are merely a few crystals you might start with while looking for options to soothe your stress and anxiety. Doing your own search in crystal shops and online is the best way to find the ones that are truly suited to you. And frankly, just because a certain crystal is used for a certain effect doesn't mean it'll work with your energy. If you pick up a stone that is supposed to make you feel calm and you feel agitated, put it down. Walk away. You're a unique flower. Make sure to take care of yourself and trust your intuition.

The next chapter will show you how to use these crystals for maximum impact by combining them with other crystals, using them in mindful ways, and targeting them to specific life issues that come up.

You'll be the one dragging your friends to crystal shops in no time.

4

MODERN RITUALS

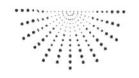

I have a vivid memory from one of my high school English classes that I think about every time I get dressed for a stressful day. It was a lesson on "arming scenes." In medieval literature, there would often be a scene where the hero would get dressed for the battle, or rescuing the princess, or slaying the dragon or whatever. He would put on his gear and muse about what was making him nervous or what was driving him to kick ass that day.

Cut to me: standing in front of my closet in my robe and slippies, trying to figure out what to put on to make me feel strong. Hmmm...

I put on a killer outfit, making sure it's comfortable, practical, and absolutely fierce. I put on professional yet feminine shoes and makeup. Next, I put on whatever crystal jewelry is calling me that day.

Then, I put my essential oil roller (with lots of stress-reducing oils) in one pocket. Then, I put the rock of the day in the other pocket. I pick up my purse and keys, and off I go—ready to slay any dragons I might meet.

Actually, let me amend that. On days where I see a lot of stress ahead, I usually choose my crystals first, then my outfit. Because, you know, priorities. That way everything matches, and I get the color theme I need for the day. Flora taught me this. Have I mentioned she's a genius?

This chapter will go through some of the ways to arm yourself—ways you can use your crystals to best effect—practices to bolster your confidence, and practices to help you deal with the hard stuff.

This makes me think of a story from my crystal journey, when I was forced to deal with some... stuff... and crystals rescued me.

Okay. If you are prone to anxiety, you know that some of the sudden memories that flash into your brain might not always be as positive as my mundane English class experience. This brings us back to the topic of trauma, which we touched on a little bit earlier in this book. Trauma is part of the magnificent wiring in our minds that reminds us of the unpleasant things we've encountered in the past to make sure we protect ourselves in the present.

These traumas can be tiny, like scraping your

knee when you were 4, which you only think about when you see a playground. Or they can be a paralyzing fear of leaving the house after getting mugged. But, to be a human is to be traumatized. I'm not sure I realized that until recently.

Soon after my trip to the crystal shop (and the wine bar) that changed my life, I threw my back out, which is the worst! One of the ways I had been endeavoring to deal with my high-stress life was to exercise. Exercise actually really helps my anxiety, but when your body breaks down, even temporarily, it's tough to do anything, let alone go to the gym. The primary method I had used to cheer myself up, exercise, was no longer available. (Obviously, I think exercise is still a good way to ease your stress and anxiety, but you're far better off with several practices in your arsenal, especially if you happen to have a bad back.)

I'd had this lower-back problem before, and I hadn't had much luck with chiropractors or physical therapists, so I went out of my comfort zone and went to see an acupuncturist. She had a wall full of diplomas. And a cabinet full of crystals!

She's the only acupuncturist I've ever been to, so I don't know if this is the typical procedure: she talked to me for about half an hour about my physical symptoms and how my emotions either helped or hindered my body. I wasn't used to people asking me those kinds of questions, so I quietly cried through the process. This is classic "me" behavior.

I was touched that the acupuncturist cared, and I was finally expressing some of the deep frustrations I was having and linking my emotions to how they manifested themselves in my body. It felt like there were deep, deep, *deep* emotions stored in my body that suddenly had permission to come out.

She handed me a crystal, a Black Tourmaline, and she told me I could hold it while we continued talking. Black Tourmaline reduces worry, as I mentioned. It soothes negative thoughts. It's incredibly comforting. But on this occasion, it loosened some old trauma that, apparently, was finally ready for release.

During the following hour, while I was getting my treatment (still blubbering on and off), the acupuncturist talked me through a bunch of philosophies I knew nothing about (at the time). She described why she was putting needles near the locations of specific chakras. She asked if it was okay to lay Clear Quartz on my back while she worked; it helped both of us focus on the healing, and it helped energized the body to speed up the process. I never even considered that crystals could be used in this way; It was an amazing and eye-opening session.

When I got home from the session, I cried some more. Hard. And after crying myself into a nap and waking up after a few hours…I felt like a new person. The next day I felt even better. It's like a dam had burst after a long time, and all the debris was washing away. Oh, and my back was better. Wow.

I bring this story up to say that, of course, simply holding a crystal is a great way to connect to the energy of the crystal, but that's just the very beginning of how people use crystals for healing. In this chapter, we'll talk about some of those ways.

More specifically, though, crystals can be used for releasing trauma we might have literally stored in our bodies for safekeeping. I learned later that the lower back, which is the part of my back I usually throw out, represents feeling supported (or not supported, as the case may be). Since it's associated with the sacral chakra, it also has to do with support regarding relationships, money, or creative pursuits.

I started paying attention and noticed that every time I threw my back out, it happened to coincide with times in my life when I lacked support: at work, at home, in my friendships. I started discussing some of these things with my therapist. I didn't really go into the details of crystals or energy with him—I didn't want him to think I was an *absolute* crazy person. I just brought it up as a talking point when he asked me how I'd been doing. It's almost like my crystal journey has led me, step by step, to delve into some things that were still bothering me even though I didn't realize they were still there.[1]

Your body remembers things, even if your brain doesn't. The sacral chakra develops between 3 and 7 years of age, a particularly vulnerable time in human development. No matter how hard your parents try, it's almost impossible for you to escape that tender age without a few bumps and bruises (literal and figurative). I had very good parents, but they weren't perfect. They yelled fairly often. School tended to be awful for this sensitive nerd—although there were good moments, I suppose.

To a seven-year-old, even the most minor thing can feel devastating. And your body can store that stuff away for later use, just to make absolutely sure you avoid similar situations in the future. That's why, when there is conflict at work, sometimes it feels overwhelming, like I want to quit my job, change my name, and flee the country. Or if I have even a small fight with my husband, I get terrified of him leaving me, and I descend into a panic attack. My mom and I still argue sometimes over the dumbest crap, and I hate it. Sometimes, the chaos threatens to overtake me.

And this is just one chakra! Now imagine how these things are compounded when you consider the number of chakras you have and how each of them is an intelligent energy center working nonstop to

CRYSTALS FOR THE MIND

keep you alive. There's a good chance *most* of your chakras have stored at least one trauma. In my case, it was *all* of them, at first. I've cleared lots of them now, but it's a lifelong process. And a rewarding one.

I know some of you reading this right now had absolutely awful childhoods and even serious traumas later in life that have left you with major scars (again, both literal and figurative). I, too, have had some... stuff... that has been an absolute nightmare to deal with, both as a child and as an adult.

You might be surprised how many people around you have had really awful experiences—we just don't talk about them because it's so stigmatized. It makes us feel like we're the only ones who have ever had terrible stuff happen to them, but it's just not true. Everybody has stuff that scars them, whether it's classified by other people as "big" or not. Sometimes we go through stuff that seems little but is, in fact, big. And, sometimes we go through huge stuff; it affects us more than we can possibly express to anyone, no matter how hard we try.[2]

When the acupuncturist was talking to me (in a very vulnerable position—shirtless on a table with, like, a thousand needles in my back), I realized that some of the stuff I thought I had dealt with was *still very much with me.* The needles plus the crystals she'd placed on me seemed to help get it out, to unburden me. Even though I hadn't been aware of it, these traumas were stuck in my body and mounting over time, like aging a fine and stinky, stinky cheese. (That was gross. Sorry.)

Energy theory teaches us that when we release trauma from our physical bodies, we can gain some healing by not having to carry it anymore. And crystals, it turns out, are a great way to release old energy in a highly accessible, do-it-yourself way. You don't necessarily need an acupuncturist or a healer. This is something you can do right now.

So, without dwelling too much more on the details of my life, let's start to look at how you can actually get the most out of your crystals. I've shared these stories so you can relate to my experience, perhaps, and maybe see yourself in the way I've dealt with my stress and anxiety using crystals.

As you get into the nitty-gritty, be gentle with yourself. We'll talk more about self-care in a little while. For now, though, here are a few ways to use crystals and in various levels of difficulty.

LEVEL 1: EASY DOES IT

Let's start with the most obvious way to use crystals: wearing them as jewelry.

Your favorite crystal stores (online and in-person) will probably be filled with crystal jewelry. This is one of my favorite ways to use crystals. It's

CRYSTALS FOR THE MIND

easy, convenient, and—duh—crystals are pretty! Crystal jewelry makes a statement about your personal commitments to honoring yourself and the universe. Plus, it can connect you with other crystal practitioners when they see you wearing crystals in public. Personally, I love to see other crystal folks when I'm out and about. I hardly ever have an impulse to speak to strangers—I'm an introvert—but there's something about seeing a Rose Quartz around someone's neck that makes me want to strike up a conversation!

Crystal jewelry comes in all kinds of varieties and styles, including masculine, feminine, and gender-neutral. I like necklaces because they are perfectly positioned near my throat, heart, and solar plexus chakras, but bracelets and earrings are also helpful. Earrings are especially nice for the third eye and crown chakras. (My go-to weekday earrings are Amethyst.) If you like using essential oils, they make both bracelets and necklaces with diffuser stones on them so you can add aromatherapy to your crystals. You can also make your own jewelry by purchasing (or ordering) crystal beads in bulk and stringing them together on your own. I've even thrown little jewelry-making parties with my friends and some wine; it's super relaxing, and you have a fun item to wear when you're done.

The second most convenient way to use crystals

is to put them in a pocket, or, if you don't have a pocket, sticking them in your bra. (See Chapter 1.) Actually, after I started writing this book, I found out that they now make bras with small loops on them for the express purpose of putting a crystal there. Yes, I'll take seven, please—one for every day of the week.

For you non-bra wearers out there, if you find another good way to do this, let me know. I have tried wearing crystals in my waistband or inside my leggings... and they fall out almost immediately. I suggested my husband put a crystal in his sock when he was running a 5K, but it got into his sneaker before the starting pistol. But he did carry it in his hand.

Of course, you can always just put a crystal or two in your pocket if your clothes are handy enough to contain pockets. I'm a huge fan of clothes with pockets, myself. Sometimes if two or three varieties of crystal are calling to me on a particular day, putting them in my pocket is the best option because there's plenty of space. Keeping a crystal on your person this way is helpful because it's a little less "obvious" than wearing it as jewelry, and it allows you to combine the properties of multiple crystals for maximum effect. You can also keep crystals in your purse or wallet, especially if they are too bulky to fit (or thin enough to go in your billfold).

The third easy way to use crystals is to use them as home decor. Crystals come in all kinds of shapes and sizes, and mine have slowly overtaken our apartment. My husband often comes home to find that the mailguy has delivered yet another large glittering hunk of rock. I set them on side tables, on shelves, and on kitchen counters. I also use them as desk ornaments, paperweights, and curios. You can also buy crystals that come with a light beneath them to use as a lamp. These provide gentle, soft lighting that radiates good vibes. I love using only a crystal light for a few minutes before bed to let my eyes adjust gradually to the darkness and wind down for the night. I sometimes also use them as a nightlight—some of them come with a dimmer switch, which I absolutely adore.

LEVEL 2: GETTING A LITTLE FANCYPANTS

Those last few methods are the most straightforward ways to use crystals without getting too complicated. Let's look at a few more complex ways, though, which can boost your crystal abilities when you use them regularly. Get as fancy or simple as you like; all methods are valid and can be really helpful. Use your intuition to know what's best suited to your needs.

The more complex ways to use crystals involve

deliberately combining crystals in intentional ways. For instance, if you want to combine unconditional love with speaking your truth, you might put a Rose Quartz with an Aquamarine. You can put them in your pocket or purse together or build a crystal grid, which I'll explain in a moment. I also sometimes put several crystals in a small cloth bag—helpfully, crystals often come in a nice little pouch when you order them online—and hang the bag on my bedpost or put it in my purse.

Here's a recipe for a crystal bag I've got right now: one Selenite heart, four Rose Quartz, and an Aquamarine. I set an intention with them for clarity and love while working on my projects, and I keep them near me while I work. I've also sometimes put crystal bags under my bed, in a drawer, in a suitcase, or in other handy places where they can discreetly carry out their work.

You can also arrange crystals in what is called a crystal grid. It's a combination of crystals in a specific pattern designed to let them work together in harmony for greater strength. You can create a crystal grid out of that recipe I just shared, actually. Take the Selenite heart and place it in the center of where you want your grid (a side table or shelf works well, so it's out of the way). Next, place the four Rose Quartz around it, one on each side (top, bottom, left, and right). Lastly, intuitively place the

CRYSTALS FOR THE MIND

Aquamarine where it feels good to you. Stand back and admire your work. You might wish to place one hand over the grid to feel the energy of it. Often, crystals are more powerful arranged this way.

The internet is full of crystal grid layout patterns you can print off if you want a guideline to keep your lines straight. I tend to just use my intuition, though. The choice is yours. As you can see, I'm sharing some recipes and ideas with you, but remember that you should always use your intuition. You know what you need much more than I do. Feel free to try mine and see, though. Then, tweak as needed.

When creating grids, you want to make sure they're not going to be disturbed because they are more effective when they stay in the original pattern you set. Of course, if one of them gets knocked out of whack (by a pet or a family member), you can easily re-do the crystal grid. It's actually really fun and rewarding to re-do the grid from time to time; it's a relaxing, meditative experience. Still, if you don't have time to constantly re-do your grid, keep it in a safe place. My husband won't admit that he likes to re-arrange them from time to time, almost like a Zen garden. I just let him get on with it. (Incidentally, if you have a Zen garden, it's so fun to replace the usual stones with crystals, instead).

Speaking of meditating, meditation is another

really common way to use crystals. You can simply hold a chosen crystal in your hand while meditating or even use it as a visual focus to look at for the duration of your meditation. You can also arrange crystals on or around your body while meditating, which can be a really powerful experience. You can do this by chakra or by intuition, but if you choose to use chakras, here are the locations:

1. **Crown chakra:** On or near the top of your head (Clear Quartz, Lithium Quartz, Howlite, Selenite)
2. **Third Eye chakra:** On the forehead or next to the ears (Amethyst, Violet Fluorite, Lepidolite)
3. **Throat chakra:** On the throat or next to the neck (Blue Lace Agate, Amazonite, Chrysocolla, Aquamarine)
4. **Heart chakra:** On the chest or to the side near the arms (Malachite, Rose Quartz, Bloodstone, Emerald)
5. **Solar plexus chakra:** On the belly, below the ribcage, or beside the body nearby (Citrine, Pyrite, Tiger's Eye, Amber)
6. **Sacral chakra:** On the lower belly or beside the body nearby (Carnelian, Moonstone, Kyanite)
7. **Root chakra:** On the hips, thighs, legs,

feet, or beside the body near these areas (Black Tourmaline, Lava Stone, Hematite, Red Jasper, Smoky Quartz)

This can be done on the front or back, although it would be helpful to have a friend or family member assist with your back (just so you can reach).[3]

If you visit a Reiki practitioner, they might place crystals on or around your body while they work; this can be a powerfully cleansing and relaxing experience. Or, if you go to an acupuncturist who uses crystals (like I did), they might place crystals on various parts of the body or even use them to massage acupressure points during the session. Not all acupuncturists use crystals, so do some research and see if there's one in your area who provides this service. There are also practitioners who provide crystals-only services, in fact, so look around and see who you can find. You can do a lot of it on your own though, by simply meditating with the crystals on the chakras. Just focus in and see what comes up. Soft music, aromatherapy, candles, and a quiet space can help you hone in.

You can set lots of other intentions with crystal meditations, such as health, wealth, relationships, and almost anything you can think of. A really simple one you can do is a new moon ritual to set an intention for the coming month. Since the moon is in partnership with you (just like everything else in the universe), its energy-pull is powerful all the time, but especially at the new and full moon phases. At the new moon, burn some incense or sage, light some candles, and set up a crystal grid. Write down your intentions for the next month—whatever you want more of in the coming month, focus on it at the new moon. Then, over the month, notice how these things are infused into your daily activities. For instance, if you want to work on speaking your truth, use throat chakra stones and write down ways that you are working on truth in your life. After doing this, you might start to notice opportunities to live authentically showing up; you might find it gets easier to be yourself without trying.

Similarly, you can do the same thing at the full moon, which is when your new moon intentions start to bear fruit. Set up your space like before, and this time write down everything that has manifested for you since the new moon. Keep doing this over a few months, adjusting your crystals and your intentions as you move forward. You can use a new topic every month or stick to the same topic for a while until you feel satisfied with your progress in it; just do what feels right.

LEVEL 3: BEING A LITTLE BIT WITCHY WITH IT

If this is all starting to sound a bit like magick[4], you would be right. Here's an example of crystal usage that falls more in the category of Wicca or witchcraft, if that's what you're into. There are thousands of spells you can use with crystals, so I won't spend too much time on them here. You can do your own research to find the ones that serve your needs, but here's one to whet your appetite:

A grounding and centering herb jar:[5]

Take 1 tablespoon each of sage, lavender, and sandalwood or patchouli and gently mix them in a mortar and pestle (or a bowl and spoon). With each herb, say something like, "Sage, thank you for grounding and centering me from within this jar. Blessed be." Once all the herbs are mixed, pour them into a glass jar.

Then, take 3 pieces of hematite into your two hands and take a moment to ground yourself into the earth, feeling how they keep you centered and calm.

Lastly, place the hematite into the jar with the herbs and say, "From now on, this jar returns me to the Earth and to my center. Blessed be."

Keep the jar in a sacred place (such as an altar or

meditation space) and open it to smell the herbs to bring you back to your center.

You can also use incantations and spells like this when creating crystal grids or bags or boxes. If you're into it, take a deep dive into all the ways you can use crystals this way for powerful healing. The internet is full of Wiccan groups and communities. I've found these people to be really kind and generous—good company to keep.

Another way you can get a little mystical with crystals is by using pendulums. A crystal pendulum is a crystal point on a long chain, which you can use to ask questions from the universe and receive answers from the movement of the crystal.

If you're thinking this sounds a little bit like a Ouija board... you're sort of getting the idea, but not quite. Some people interpret pendulums as receiving spiritual guidance from angels or other spirit guides. Others suggest that it's just your energy answering things for you, like muscle testing in kinesiology. Personally, I think it's a combination of the two, and perhaps one day we'll understand it on a scientific level. You can decide what you believe.

I could write an entire book on using pendulums, which multiple people have done, by the way.[6] For now, here's a basic overview. I love doing this if I'm wrestling with personal questions that I have trouble answering on my own. People have used them to find water deep underground or even predict future events, which you are more than welcome to try when you get good at it. It takes a little practice, but it can be so much fun!

First, you will want to make sure your pendulum crystal is cleansed and ready to go (more on cleansing in the next chapter). Then, make sure you are feeling grounded and clear, as negativity sometimes skews the results. Next, take a brief moment to connect to the crystal by holding it in your hand and tuning into its energy. When you're ready, hold the pendulum in your dominant hand and allow the chain to dangle below your hand.

After that, you will need to do a couple of test questions to get into the zone. I usually ask the crystal to show me "yes," and then "no," so I know we're on the same page. Usually, when I ask the crystal to show me "yes," it's a clockwise motion; "no" is usually counterclockwise. However, sometimes it's back and forth for "yes" and side to side for "no" or vice versa. It can differ from person to person, so don't get too hung up on this part. You just need to be clear on what is "yes" and what is "no" so you and the crystal are on the same wavelength. Then, ask it something like, "Is today Wednesday?" or something to make sure you and the crystal are connecting.

As I said, this usually works best for me when it's a question I know that, deep down, I probably already know the answer to; it's just buried with social expectations or fears. You'll find that answers are more clear and direct when the question pertains directly to you or your role in a relationship or situation. If you get too many other players involved, sometimes the answers get muddy.[7] Some questions you might start with:

- Is ____ diet good for me?
- Is ____ purchase a worthwhile investment?
- Do I genuinely want to do ___?

One of my grandmother's sisters on the Italian side of my family was famous for predicting the sex of a baby with a pendulum. I never got to witness this, but she would put the woman's wedding ring (with a diamond usually—a crystal) on a chain and dangle it over the woman's belly. She was rumored to be very good; you could feel safe buying the mother-to-be a pink or blue outfit for her new baby.[8]

Another witchy thing you can do is learn about your Zodiac sign and its properties, and choose crystals to work with your astrology. This is another area with thousands of years of knowledge and

CRYSTALS FOR THE MIND

history, so if you want to get good at it, find books and online resources to get you started. Just like everything else, crystals are in partnership with all matter, including the stars and planets. Certain planets vibrate with certain frequencies, and you can find and use crystals to match. For example, Saturn has a strong, powerful frequency like Tiger's Eye, and Venus naturally goes with Rose Quartz.

When certain planets are in power in the heavens, you will probably find yourself more drawn to these crystals, or you can use them deliberately to align yourself with the power of the planets. I'm a Leo, so fiery crystals like citrine and carnelian are really supportive to me. That being said, sometimes my Leo-ness feels like it's overcompensating, so at those times, I mindfully pick a more calming water-type crystal (such as Aquamarine) to balance myself out.

The final thing I want to discuss in this chapter is making crystal elixirs, which I mentioned in the first chapter, if you recall. By putting certain crystals in water, you can then drink that water and receive the benefits of the crystal that way. Not only does it help to cleanse any negative vibes that might be in water (and tap water is always risky for that), it gives the added benefit of whatever properties you want whenever you take a drink.

As I said, some crystals aren't safe for drinking

water, so always, always, *always* look them up first, so you avoid harmful toxins. Still, here are a few that are safe for water and really helpful:

- Rose Quartz
- Clear Quartz
- Smoky Quartz
- Amethyst

You can purchase one of those fancy crystal water bottles or just put the crystal in a jar for a few hours or overnight. My favorite elixir method is to put some crystals and some tap water in a large glass jar then set it on a sunny windowsill for a few hours. The water will taste better and feel better in your mouth when you're done, not to mention it will have let go of all kinds of harmful impurities. I love the way elixirs taste, and in fact, I rarely enjoy tap water anymore. I'm spoiled, I guess.

If you're not sure about a crystal or want to be super safe, you can also put a smaller glass jar filled with a crystal or two into a bigger jar filled with water. That way, the crystals never actually touch the water but can still help. You can also use elixirs as a room spray or aura mist instead.

I recently started watering my houseplants with elixir water too. The houseplants make the oxygen that my husband, my dog, and I breathe every day. Why not nourish them with the best water I can?[9]

These practices are just the tip of the iceberg. I'm continually impressed with the innovative ways people work crystals into their daily rituals. These practices are a great way to get started, but you'll never stop learning new things you can use your crystals for.

5

USING CRYSTALS TO SOOTHE YOUR
STRESS AND ANXIETY

At the beginning of this book, I went over the ways that stress and anxiety disrupt my life and asked you to do the same by writing down your experiences. In this chapter, I will go more in-depth about how my crystal-related self-care assists me with the things I mentioned earlier. No doubt, your stress-and-anxiety and my stress-and-anxiety share some similar symptoms, but no two people are the same. Steal my practices if they resonate with you! But I'll also give you ideas for practices that address all of the common symptoms of anxiety and stress.

Take notes! Write down anything that sounds like it might help you. By the end of this chapter, you'll have a list of things to try. Even if only a few of these ideas work for you, you'll be well on your way to having a robust self-care action plan that will make a giant difference in your life. This is my promise to you.

*

To begin, here are the particular struggles that I told you I deal with on a regular basis, connected with my anxiety and stress:

SELF-EXPRESSION

You might remember that lack of self-expression is a biggie for me. I still have the Blue Lace Agate that started this whole journey. (It's right by my keyboard while I type this.) I also treated myself to an Amazonite pendant that I saw online. Amazonite is another crystal that helps you live your truth. I wear it around my neck, so it's close to my heart and close to my throat. I'm touching it right now, finding the courage to type this. Because these crystals are both throat chakra crystals, they work wonderfully with self-expression and clearing anxiety there.

A similar stone could resonates with your own self-expression issues. No matter who you are, you probably struggle to express yourself from time to time. Perhaps you struggle with it every day. A crystal can be a powerful reminder of the true you, just waiting to come out.

You will probably run across a variety of throat chakra crystals in your journey. (See also: Turquoise, Blue Kyanite, and Aquamarine.) The nice thing about stones for self-expression is that they affect so many other aspects of your life: your relationships, your career, your health, everything. When you can know and express your needs, your whole life flows better.

Personally, when I have my throat chakra stones, I can write more quickly and easily, and I'm not as worried about what people will think. I don't hesitate over every sentence, and I feel confident that what I'm saying is more authentic to the real me.

I have absolutely had creative projects that I could not even begin properly. I'd start, stop, give up, try again... And then I'd go set up a crystal grid, including every blue crystal in my collection. Usually, once I did that, the project began to flow! I'd get more compliments too because people could see that it was my authentic work, instead of me trying to follow someone else's vision. Think blue!

DIGESTIVE UPSET

Another thing that anxiety gives me is an upset stomach. Any stressful situation is sure to leave me in cramps, and probably unable to eat anything until it's over and I have time to debrief and calm down

CRYSTALS FOR THE MIND

again. When you think of digestive pain, you might go to Citrine or Carnelian—these are great for that purpose. But I stumbled upon Amber. Amber is not technically a crystal; it's a fossilized resin. But it's been used in healing for generations.

Years ago, when my grandfather died, my mother and I went through some of his things. He had an amber ring, set in very cheap-looking gold—which didn't match his personality at all! I can't imagine him ever wearing it. But he had it and kept it safe in a box. I asked my mom if I could take it. Once I started learning about healing crystals, I pulled it out again. This was an instance of the crystal finding me instead of the other way around. Now, how was I going to use it?

Some quick research will tell you that Amber is related to both the sacral and solar plexus chakras and has been known to help with digestion. I don't wear the ring (have I mentioned it's really ugly?), but I do put it in my pocket quite often when I anticipate a big stress or big decision. It makes me feel stronger. And it makes me feel closer to my grandfather. To use one of his favorite phrases, it gives me "intestinal fortitude!"

By working with chakras that assist digestion in conjunction with crystals, you can greatly impact any tummy troubles you might have. More specifically, you can work on the particular causes of your personal tummy troubles and allow crystals to assist. For instance, if you're looking for more *flow* in your life (if you catch my drift), you might look for crystals that release blockages and promote movement, such as water-element crystals. Aventurine, anyone? If your digestive issues coincide with you feeling ungrounded, some grounding crystals will help. Hematite, perhaps. You can use trial and error and intuition to figure out what will be best for you, personally. Amber, though, would be a great place to start.

OVERALL WELLNESS/BODY CARE

As I mentioned, crystals have brought really powerful changes in how I take care of myself in general. I've noticed that I take more joy in my body-care routines when there are crystals involved. I love pampering myself with crystals because I know the benefits will last beyond the treatment (since crystals improve your energetic makeup over time). There are actually lots of ways to incorporate crystals into your regular activities. I've got herbal teas infused with crystal energy, candles that contain crystals (when they burn down, just wash them and use them!), and even beauty products. Here are a few body-care ideas to get you started:

A simple ritual you can do with crystals is to take

CRYSTALS FOR THE MIND

a bath. Get some scented bath salts, essential oils, candles, music, flowers, a face mask, and whatever else you use to pamper yourself. Then, place your chosen crystals around the edge of the tub or in the water, if it's a safe crystal to use in water (make sure to research each one to be sure it's safe!).

Taking a crystal ritual bath at the new moon (like I mentioned before) is a beneficial thing to do if you want to fill the upcoming month with more of what you want. My husband has basically learned this routine; in fact, he's started to just turn on the tub at 8pm on the new moon if he happens to notice the moon phase. (I guess he's more supportive than I think. Thanks, babe!).

You can also place herbal tea bags in the water to enhance the experience and soak in some healing properties through your skin. For instance, lavender tea with Amethyst would be an excellent combination for unconditional love and serenity. If you use a detox bath salt, you will purge all kinds of harmful toxins and feel so much better. Personally, I sleep much better after taking a detox bath, and I wake up feeling lighter.

When I get ready for bed in the evening, I often spritz myself, my room, and my bed with scented crystal elixir to sluff off the negative energy I might have picked up throughout my day. If I've been out in public with noisy or angsty people, I don't want that energy sticking to me any longer than necessary, especially when I sleep. Sometimes I hold a Selenite wand and move it through my aura to do the same thing, but a spray bottle filled with elixir is a bit easier to use, and it smells nice with the oils in it, too.

Have you seen those facial rollers made of Rose Quartz? They're handy tools designed to stimulate your skin and improve circulation for a healthy, youthful glow. They come in a few other stone types and are very affordable. I also have a *gua sha* tool (a Chinese self-massage tool) made from Rose Quartz. I use these on my face after I wash and moisturize every night. It feels fantastic, and it really helps keep my skin clear. You can use a *gua sha* tool on the rest of your body, too, to help with cellulite, circulation, and just general wellness. Do a little research on this one, as there's a bit of a technique to it. However, I learned it easily enough! Usually, I dry-brush my skin with a soft bristle brush before getting into the shower, then use the *gua sha* on my arms, legs, and torso while I'm in the shower. By the time I've used my body scrub and moisturized with a Rose Quartz infused body cream, I feel like a million bucks. They also make massage rollers out of crystals if you prefer that particular shape and size. Rolling your skin with a massage roller made out of Selenite brings out negative energies in a powerful way.

CRYSTALS FOR THE MIND

I also have several makeup and hair products that have been infused with crystals, and I love the way they look and feel. For example, I've got a body butter made with aloe, sugar, and literal ground-up Carnelian! When I found out that was a thing, I immediately whipped out my credit card; take my money! It feels incredible on my skin, and it makes me feel amazing, too.

Still, if your budget is tight, you can get similar benefits with your very own DIYs. The internet is full of ideas, but my personal favorite is getting an essential oil roller that contains crystals. (You can also purchase the components and make it yourself.) By pouring the essential oils on the crystals, you benefit from both the crystals and the oils. I keep a crystal oil roller in my bedside cabinet and use it every night (it's Amethyst, plus some calming oils for sleep).

Another thing you can do is to simply set a crystal with your beauty products and let it cleanse them and infuse them. Here's an idea: take one part shea butter, one part coconut oil, and a few of your favorite essential oils. Whip them together in an empty jar using a fork, then set a Rose Quartz on top overnight. In the morning, you'll have a glorious body butter with all kinds of goodness in it. Pick some essential oils that match your needs, but also go with the crystal you choose. For instance, I love to pair rose essential oil or rose water with Rose Quartz. It just has a nice vibe.

SELF-DOUBT IN RELATIONSHIPS

You might recall how anxiety makes me second-guess all my relationships. Ouch, this one is hard to admit, but it's one of the toughest struggles I have in my life. Well, for this, my go-to crystal is Rose Quartz. Rose Quartz is the crystal of compassion and unconditional love. I can't get enough Rose Quartz in my life; I give it as a gift several times a year! (Mental note: Send Flora some Rose Quartz.) My prized piece is a gorgeous obelisk of Rose Quartz, which I keep in the meditation nook in my house. If I'm sitting, I rest it in my lap. If I'm lying down, I rest it on my heart.

I repeat personal mantras. I master my breath. I try to stay present. And the crystal helps me focus on compassion for myself and others. This kind of meditation is powerful for me, and when I'm finished, I'm calm and ready for anything.

Some other good crystals for unconditional love are Lepidolite and basically any heart chakra crystal. I already mentioned that heart chakra crystals tend to make me cry. This is just one way that crystals can bring up old emotions for cleansing. I often legitimately set aside time to meditate with heart chakra crystals and allowed myself a good cry. It's a release my body craves, and it's always really cleansing.[1]

When dealing with deep-seated trauma, such as childhood abuse or significant violence, you can allow crystals to gently pull the energetic components out of your body without needing to "deal" with it on a surface level. For me, talking to my therapist about stuff that has happened is really helpful, but it's also traumatizing to even speak to him about it; it drags everything up all over again. Therapy helps to get it out, but then I go home sometimes more upset and need a long time to put myself back together again. That's why I routinely set aside time to let *my crystals* pull the old emotions out energetically. It means there's less I have to wrestle with on the surface.

Using crystals in this way helps me let the trauma out on a visceral level, rather than having to view it on the mental and emotional levels again. Although it's sometimes a bit uncomfortable, it feels much better afterward. And I notice that my whole life gets better a few days after one of these sessions. It brings a sense of underlying calm that I didn't have before. It's almost like pulling out a splinter—it hurts, but then it gets better. It's like a detox for your soul.

✶

Of course, my stress and anxiety symptoms barely scratch the surface of the experiences we all share. They're good examples, but definitely not the only ones people experience. Here are a few more that you might apply to you, and here's what to do about them. As you learn more about crystals, you'll be able to mix and match your symptoms and your crystals in creative ways to help yourself through tough moments.

DIFFICULTY SLEEPING

Sleep troubles are some of the most significant problems anxiety causes, in my opinion, because if you can't sleep... you can't really do anything else, either. How stressful!

I've already mentioned some nighttime rituals that assist me with sleeping well. Still, I want to go a little further into it by talking about grounding some more. I've mentioned grounding briefly throughout this book, but I can't overstate its importance—both in your overall health in general and your mental health specifically. Grounding improves your connection with the earth, which is where all crystals come from incidentally. Root chakra stones are grounding, so anything black, red, or brown is an excellent option (such as Black Tourmaline, Hematite, Lava Stone, Red Jasper, Smoky Quartz, etc.).

If you suffer from nightmares, use cleansing stones like Selenite and Clear Quartz to protect your aura at night from negative energies that can influence your dreams. Amethyst can also assist with better dreams, as negative energies in the third eye can be a source of bad dreams. And staring into a piece of Lepidolite is like looking into the vastness of the universe; it can't help but calm you. It's the perfect thing to send you off to dreamland.

FEELING TIRED OR WEAK

Fatigue is absolutely frustrating because it feels like it'll never end. For tiredness, I usually attack it from two angles. First, I'll use stones to help me get better sleep in the first place (such as Lepidolite, Black Tourmaline, and Selenite). Since weakness or tiredness is ultimately the body crying out for more sleep, this is the most obvious first step. Then, since better sleep isn't always possible, I'll also use energizing stones like Citrine or Tiger's Eye during the day to help me feel more awake and alert.

Keep in mind, of course, that the stones that are energizing for me might be calming for you (and vice versa), so experiment until you know what works. Some energizing stones, too, actually make me feel jittery or frantic, like I just chugged a triple-shot iced mocha, so watch out for that yourself. As usual, combining stones with others can balance them out to keep them from being too intense and can also strengthen their healing benefits.[2]

NEGATIVE THOUGHTS

Depending on the "flavor" of your negative thoughts, different stones might work, but my go-to crystals for negativity are Clear Quartz and Selenite. These stones cleanse negative thoughts and make space for newer, clearer thoughts. Black Tourmaline and Hematite are good protective stones that can ward off other people's negativity, too.

I also really like stones that support unconditional love, such as Amethyst and Rose Quartz. These stones can counteract negative notions both before and after they happen by filling you with positive thoughts. If your negative thoughts center around a phobia or fear, try some stones that tap into that specific need (such as Tiger's Eye for confidence, Blue Lace Agate for social anxiety, or Lepidolite for overthinking).

FEELING AGITATED

Generally, agitation comes either from being ungrounded or from having negativity in your aura. If you're agitated, try grounding with root chakra stones such as Black Tourmaline, Hematite, Red Jasper, Bloodstone, Smoky Quartz, or Lava Stone. By bringing you back to your center, they'll help you feel more rooted in the earth and less likely to be pulled off balance. A number of cleansing, calming stones help with agitation too, such as Clear Quartz, Lepidolite, Moonstone, Chrysocolla, Violet Fluorite, Selenite, and Howlite. These stones typically work by cleansing agitation from your system and can be paired with grounding stones to balance your energy.

The conventional solution for agitation is meditation, which I wholeheartedly endorse and practice myself. Meditation can take as long as a few deep breaths, or you can get a free guided meditation app and spend an hour. All of this is great, but goose your meditation practice with a healing crystal and watch the effects multiply.

DIFFICULTY CONCENTRATING

Sometimes difficulty concentrating comes from a lack of groundedness, too, so grounding stones come in handy here (Black Tourmaline, Lava Stone). However, difficulty concentrating can also stem from not living your truth or disconnection from your spiritual gifts. That is, if you're having trouble concentrating on something, that's probably your subconscious mind whispering, "This thing you're trying to work on? Yeah, it's not really what you want to do, is it?"[3]

Of course, sometimes you have to do things you don't want to do, so at those times, try a throat chakra stone (Blue Lace Agate, Amazonite, Chrysocolla, Aquamarine) to align yourself with your personal truth in the task at hand, a sacral chakra stone (Kyanite or Carnelian) to boost productivity and creativity, or a solar plexus stone (Citrine, Pyrite, or Tiger's Eye) to boost confidence and empowerment. You might benefit from a combination of these three chakras with some grounding stones in a productivity grid to help you focus.

This would be a great time to get a silk bag—the kind that maybe came in the mail when you ordered crystals online—and mix them together to keep you company. Put a few of these crystals together, and keep them in your purse. Or rest them on your planner! See what calm comes from the intention of concentration.

IRRITABILITY

Honestly, if I'm irritated, it's usually because I have a hidden need that needs to be met, and my body is trying to give me a little hint to take care of it. It

CRYSTALS FOR THE MIND

might be that I'm hungry or need a nap, or somebody said something to me that bothered me, and I haven't had the time to sit down and process it.

Usually, taking even five minutes to meet the need solves the issue, but there are a number of crystals that can support this process. I really like Lepidolite, Violet Fluorite, Clear Quartz, Lithium Quartz, Smoky Quartz, and Rose Quartz for their calming, supportive properties. If my irritability stems from pent-up emotions that just need to be purged before I can feel better, I find some time to meditate with Malachite or Emerald and let the crystals siphon off the trapped emotions. Remember that meditation for emotional detox can be an emotional rollercoaster, so be sure to set aside time to let it all out, if need be.

My mother, who is a role model of mine, can tend to be irritable. Her solution is to watch a movie (Steel Magnolias is a go-to for her) that makes her cry, which resets her system. I admit I use this technique, but for me, it's TV. I mean, try getting through an episode of Parenthood or This is Us without an emotional purge!

This kind of purge can be done with crystals and intention, and you don't even need Netflix. Use the crystals above, breathe, and experience the things that are making you upset. Cry if it feels good to you. And you'll find yourself ready for the next challenge.

*

Certainly, there are dozens of more ways that stress and anxiety affect your life—these are just the common ones. I've found, though, that crystals work holistically, for the most part. If I can find the right crystals for me and my needs, they'll generally assist with multiple symptoms at a time, which is such a relief. That way, you don't have to spend so much time chasing your symptoms around. If you have more specific symptoms tied to stress and anxiety, though, you can, of course, find crystals to assist. Learning more about crystals yourself or speaking to a crystal practitioner who can help you work with your individual needs.

6

CARING FOR YOURSELF AND YOUR CRYSTALS

Now that you know quite a bit about crystals and how to use them for stress and anxiety relief, let's talk about how to make sure your new crystal collection gets the tender, loving care it needs. Since everything in the universe is filled with life, it's important to treat your crystals as the intelligent, living beings they are—just like your dog or your cat or your houseplants.

To be honest, learning about crystals made me so much more appreciative of *everything* I have: my clothes, my food, my money, my phone, everything. Since everything is energy, it makes sense that when we treat every thing with respect, every thing will offer us more respect in return. I have found that my car works better, my shoes last longer, my phone breaks less often, and my life just generally goes better when I think of these things and myself in a mutually beneficial relationship. Like with my crystals.

If you're anything like me, chances are good that you might already have a few crystals lying around. Most of us were into rocks when we were younger, and I never cease to be surprised at how many "plain old rocks" are actually healing crystals.

Some time after I got into crystals, I was cleaning out an old drawer and found a Rose Quartz that I'd randomly saved from a childhood visit to South Dakota. Of course, when I was a kid, I had no clue what I was buying; it was just exciting to find a pink rock at a gift shop. I also had a few old jewelry items lying around that turned out to be healing stones when I learned what the gem was.

You might be the same, so find out what you already have along with buying some more. If you've got crystals but you're not sure what the stone is, there are so many beautiful books you can reference. Flip through and find the crystals that match yours and see if you can identify them.

The internet is also a great resource. You can try a reverse google image search or simply post in a forum about crystals and see if anyone can identify it. Crystal folks are usually friendly and would be

CRYSTALS FOR THE MIND

more than willing to help you out by letting you know what kind of crystal you might have dug out from the back of your jewelry box.

> I'll plug my Facebook group once again. People post photos all the time, and we all try to help you figure out what treasures you've got. You can join us at: www.facebook.com/groups/HealingCrystalsChangedMyDangLife

If you don't have any crystals yet though, you will want to start buying a few! The internet is one of my go-to sources, but make sure you are purchasing from reputable sources online. Standard internet shopping rules apply: don't give out personal information, use secure shopping and payment sites, and always check reviews.

More specifically, though, some crystals are lab-created, others are artificially dyed, and no two crystals are quite alike. If your crystals look flawless, dyed, or exactly like every other crystal in the box... it could be that you got a cheap imitation instead of the real thing. If that happens, consider trying another seller next time or asking for a refund.

On the subject of money, if a crystal has an outrageously high price tag or an insanely low one, that can be a red flag. You might remember that the first Blue Lace Agate I bought was about $6. A good rule of thumb for single rocks is about $3 to $10. Still, some stones are rarer than others. The rarer the stone, the higher the cost, of course. A Chrysocolla will cost more than a piece of Quartz.

If you are buying fancy jewelry with multiple crystals incorporated, that will cost you a little more. It's worth it though. Lots of the best crystal sellers are skilled artisans, so buying the nicer stuff will not only ensure good quality, it also supports an ancient craft. Personally, I love purchasing my crystals at festivals and fairs or on my favorite artisan's personal website. Typically, that benefits them the most and keeps those folks in business (which I am heavily invested in!). It also reduces the number of hands that handle your crystals in transit, limiting the amount of negative vibes that sometimes cling to crystals when being sent through the mail. I'll teach you how to cleanse negativity from crystals in a moment, but keep that in mind when purchasing online.

Etsy.com is full of exceptional artisans who want to share their crystal love with you. It's also a fantastic place to buy gifts. I've bought crystals from Amazon and from a tiny online shop in the Appalachians. The tiny-shop crystals have more power to me.[1]

CRYSTALS FOR THE MIND

You might be wondering whether it's possible for a crystal to "call" to you from an internet webpage. The answer is: absolutely. Your inner knowing will tell you which crystals you need, regardless of whether you're in person or on the other side of the globe. In fact, I have a lot of fun shopping for crystals online because it feels like more of a challenge than having crystals call to me when I walk by them in a shop. (Although that's always a blast, too. Crystals are always fun, to be perfectly honest.)

More importantly, buying crystals is fun because crystal people are giving, loving souls; it's rare that they don't sneak in an extra crystal or surprise gift in the bag when they ship it. Usually, they wrap your crystals in beautiful, practical packaging that can be re-used for crystal storage or charm bags. That's part of why I'm such a loyal customer (besides wanting to keep the crystal industry well-supported, for obvious reasons. I wouldn't want them to go out of business—horror of horrors!).

Once you get your crystals home, you'll need to store them someplace safe to protect their quality for years to come. And, you'll want to display them for the world to see, naturally. Crystals, in general, are best kept out of direct sunlight and away from water, so be mindful of storing them near windows and sinks. Sun and water fade and dissolve crystals over time, which is harmful to the crystals and potentially harmful to you if they leach toxins into the air or water. Amethyst, Rose Quartz, and Citrine are just a few examples of crystals that fade in sunlight. Malachite, Selenite, and Pyrite—among others—dissolve in water. Some crystals even oxidize when left indefinitely in the open air (hematite, for one, can rust if left lying around for too long... we're talking months or years, though). However, if your crystals get left in direct sunlight for a few hours or get slightly wet, don't panic. These are actually two important ways to clear crystals of negative energy, which I'm coming to in a moment.

First, though, you will want to keep some crystals out in the open for specific purposes and keep others stored safely away until you're ready to use them. I have several wooden bowls, crystal bowls, and an abalone shell that I display my crystals in, on shelves and tables out of direct sunlight. I also keep crystals in jewelry boxes and in soft cloth bags for safekeeping. Velvet, silk, and organza pouches work especially well for this. Thankfully, crystal sellers often ship crystals in a soft bag, which is why I have such an extensive collection of those bags tucked away in various parts of our home.[2] Wooden jewelry boxes, glass storage jars, and bead-sorter trays also work well for storing and organizing crystals. If you're going for the full witch vibe, there's nothing cooler than having a shelf-full of glass jars with colorful crystals inside. If you notice dirt or dust on your crystals, you can gently wipe them off with a cloth or soft brush. Keeping them in a box or jar protects them from collecting too much dust over time, as well.

After you choose your container, you'll want to think about how to organize them. Personally, I store similar crystals together and then group the colors by chakra, but use the system that makes the most sense to you. Some people like to label each crystal with the name on the outside, which can be especially helpful when you have multiple crystals with similar colors. You might also choose to write their healing properties on the label, too, so you can easily remember what each crystal is for.

As you gather more crystals into your collection, they will end up scattered all over the house—in your bedside table, in the living room, in your closet, in your purse, and who knows where else—so feel free to switch up your organization as often as you need to. Having a wide variety of crystals stored, organized, and labeled clearly, though, will be really useful when you're having a bad day and need to get to your crystals as fast as humanly possible. It's never fun to hunt for something when you're already stressed; I know this from experience.

Of course, you don't need thousands upon thousands of crystals to be a crystal gal or guy; you can stick to just a few go-to crystals that feel right to you. You might find, though, that the longer you stay on your crystal journey, the more the crystals will "find" you. So, don't sweat it. Just see what happens and enjoy the process.

Along with keeping your crystals stored safely, you'll want to keep your crystals "charged"—this is the word crystal healers use for removing old, stale energies from crystals every so often. Like people, crystals can get clogged with dense, low-vibe energy, reducing their effectiveness. Crystals lend you some of their energy, of course, but they also siphon off your negative energy simultaneously, which is so helpful. Every day I give thanks for my little rocky friends. Still, also, just like people, crystals can become overloaded with your angst, which is the crystal equivalent of burnout. An overloaded crystal feels energetically heavy, dense, or even gives off negative vibes, which is the opposite of what you want. To keep your crystals operating at their maximum capacity, give them a little vacation every so often to rest and recharge. Everything in the universe, after all, does better with a little TLC.

I try to charge my go-to crystals at least once a month, but as you get more comfortable with crystals, you'll be able to tell when a crystal needs a little

CRYSTALS FOR THE MIND

cleanse. You'll notice that they don't work quite so well for you, that you're not drawn to particular stones quite so often, or that they give you a heavy or dark feeling when you hold them. These are good signs that it's time to cleanse and charge.

I have certain grids and crystals that need to be recharged every single day because they're working so hard around the clock. Others, however, can get by with less. This becomes second nature over time, so you're sure to get the hang of it. In the meantime, you can't charge your crystals too often, so go for it.

You can charge all your crystals at the same time or just do a few at a time, depending on how many you have and what you use them for. Sometimes I cleanse individual crystals. Sometimes I do them all at once. I just decide what I have time and energy for and go with that. Charging crystals is a fun, healing experience, so I rarely think of it as a chore, like cleaning my kitchen sink is. Sure, both of them need to be done regularly, but one feels thankless, and the other one feels like I'm doing something really powerful for myself and for my home and family. It's almost like the crystals sigh with relief when I charge them. My sink has never done that (so far, anyway).

Cleansing your crystals is an intuitive process, and most crystal people will have different guidelines than I do. That's okay since different methods work for different people and different crystals. If one method doesn't work for you, try something different until you find what works the best. Here are several guidelines and instructions you can use to help your crystals function at the optimum level.

When you purchase a new crystal, be sure to cleanse it as soon as you get it home and before you start to really use it.[3] Cleanse all your crystals regularly when they are in constant use. If you store a crystal for a while and then get it back out again, you will want to cleanse it before you start using it again.

And how do you charge your crystals, you ask? Sunlight, moonlight, water, and certain other crystals will do the trick. You can rinse your crystals for a few minutes in water—tap water is fine, although filtered water tends to be more effective—or leave them in sunlight or moonlight for several hours and let the sun or moon purify them. Although some people leave theirs for up to 24 hours, seven or eight hours should be enough. Generally speaking, leaving a crystal in direct sunlight will bleach it, causing it to lose its vibrant color. When charging a crystal with the sun, just set it in sunlight for the allotted time, then move it back to its usual spot.

Moonlight is another excellent way to charge your crystals. You can set your crystals in a box on your porch or on your windowsill, where they will be in direct moonlight for most of the night. The full moon is the most potent time to do this, for obvious reasons, but other times can work as well. If it's cloudy, though, it will be less effective than pure moonlight. "The more, the merrier!" is the rule of thumb with moonlight and crystals.

My favorite way to charge my crystals is to set any clogged crystals near my Selenite tower for a few hours. And I keep a few Selenite spheres in with my crystal collection to protect them from dense energies. Various forms of Quartz will cleanse other crystals, too, but I've found that Selenite is the strongest. After all, Selenite is named after a moon goddess and resonates with the frequency of the moon, so it works powerful magic clearing crystals of negativity. Just keep Selenite all over your home. It's a really good way to repel negative energies and expel them when they inadvertently enter.

I also have a Selenite bowl that works wonders. My Selenite bowl, in fact, is almost always filled with whatever crystals I happen to be charging. Selenite comes in all shapes and sizes, such as bowls and plates and charging stations, so I recommend everyone serious about crystals look into them. You can also place small pieces of Selenite in a circle or square around a pile of crystals you want to charge, or simply pile them all together. Lots of crystal sellers offer "Selenite protection kits" or similar collections designed for energetic cleansing, so that's an efficient option if you're looking for an easy way to charge your crystals. For such an important and valuable crystal, Selenite is relatively inexpensive, so I heartily recommend finding one. Or nine.

You can also cleanse crystals by setting them on the grass or burying them in the earth for a few hours or overnight. To use this method, dig a small hole (big enough to just cover your crystals) and gently cover them with earth for a day or so.

Using natural running water such as a creek or river is a fantastic method, too, if you have access to some. Dip the crystals in your source of running water by hand, or perhaps use a net bag to submerge them for a few minutes until all the energetic gunk is cleared away.

Lastly, you can cleanse crystals with smoke. Burning incense, sage, or palo santo is a great way to cleanse your space and your crystals. Light a piece of whatever you are burning and pass it back and forth over your crystal collection a few times. Allow the smoke to cleanse the crystals for 2-3 minutes at least, or simply light the material and let it smudge the air around them until it burns out. Smoke flows wherever it needs to cleanse, so it will do what it needs to do.

Be sure to cleanse your crystal jewelry in the same way, taking care to be mindful of the other

CRYSTALS FOR THE MIND

components of your jewelry. For instance, a bracelet with metal fittings might rust if left underground or kept wet for too long, so choose a different cleansing method to be safe. If you're wearing crystals in a body piercing, you might not always remember to remove and cleanse them, so set a reminder or mark your calendar if you wear them habitually.

Keeping some Selenite in my jewelry box is often sufficient to cleanse my jewelry between uses. Still, sometimes they need a good long rest in a Selenite bowl for good measure. If I wear a crystal item for a few days in a stressful environment, I automatically know I'll need to use a stronger method, such as a lengthy Selenite cleanse or a water rinse, to do the job. This has been something I learned through trial and error as well as reading up on it, so be patient with yourself as you learn.

All in all, crystals don't require that much care compared to most other household objects. And it's usually pretty fun instead of a burden, so it's definitely worth it. If you're finding it challenging to keep your crystals charged all the time, I recommend just storing them in a Selenite bowl or in a jewelry box with Selenite and keeping them in a safe corner. That way, they'll always be charged when you get ready to use them.

If you're new to crystals, I'm going to give you two assignments: mark your calendar for the next new moon, and order a $5 piece of Selenite. See what happens when you cleanse your crystals for the first time. Something tells me cleansing will become a cherished practice for you, as it has for me and a million other crystal nerds around the globe.

CONCLUSION

Now that I've talked quite a bit about crystals and how they've really helped my anxiety and stress levels, along with how to care for your crystals and yourself, you're ready to go out and try it on your own. In this final chapter, I want to share just one more example—from early in my crystal journey—that really helped me understand crystals for self-care. It's not the only example I could tell you, but it's a good one. There are literally thousands of combinations and techniques you can use to make crystals work well for you, if you take the time to find them. This is a story about how crystals helped me understand my life, in big-picture mode.

This story takes place at the office job I had a few years ago It was one of those moments when I had worked on a massive project for a long time, pouring

CONCLUSION

my heart and soul into every little detail, then petty office politics shot the whole thing down. Well, it just so happened to also be a few days before my period. Let's just say it was a recipe for a panic attack. (M*any* tears were shed, okay?)

I pulled myself together and took care of business as best I could, but I had terrible PMS. I've had PMS off and on, and sometimes it's worse than others, but this time it was debilitatingly awful. It hurt to move. I couldn't hold down food. My head throbbed, so I couldn't see straight. What's more, *nothing* I tried worked. I took all the pills, did all the yoga, made my husband rub my feet, listened to healing music, meditated, *all* my go-to methods. Useless. I couldn't even stand up straight, so how could I go to work—which was stressful enough on a good day?

Before I learned about crystals, I would have had to call in sick, but I was a crystal girl now. I thought I'd give it a try. I went to my crystal collection, and it was Red Jasper that called to me. I immediately put one in my pocket, and *voila*...within ten minutes, the cramps disappeared. I still felt sort of crappy, but I could stand up straight and get ready for work, which was a big step forward. Grateful and slightly astonished, I endured the rest of my day, but later that night while soaking in an Epsom salt bath, I pondered how that possibly could have worked so well. I still couldn't believe a *rock* (remember, it really was early in my journey) could have worked when everything else had failed.

I googled and found out that Red Jasper is a powerful stone for menstruation and period pain. Still, I wanted to know why that particular stone was the right one for me that day, since there are dozens of other stones that assist with PMS, some of which were literally in my crystal collection sitting right next to the Jasper.

Red Jasper is a root chakra stone, I read, so it affects all the relevant body parts. Still, more importantly, it works with stability and security. That major upset at work had really thrown me for a loop; it put me on "shaky ground," so to speak. And I'd spent an entire month storing that in my root chakra as stress. No, no! As trauma!

My body was attempting to protect me. It was saying, "Work is a terribly unsafe place! You can't go there again. You should just stay home. Here, have some cramps to make *sure* you can't leave the house. You're welcome!" (Thanks, body. I owe you one?)

My physical symptoms—the stress on my body—was created *by my body* in order to care for me. But, my mind is stronger than my body gives it credit for. Spending some time with the healing energy from the Red Jasper reminded my mind that, "Girl, you got this." The feel of the crystal in my hand inter-

CONCLUSION

rupted the messages from my body to my mind, and allowed me a moment to remember my own power.

From then on, crystals have become the *first* thing I turn to for PMS instead of the last thing. (Although I usually still take Advil, because, ouch, some pains are just unavoidable. Manageable, but unavoidable.)

I guess I'm saying that crystals gave me the option of choosing to offer myself compassion for my stress and anxiety. Because it's not my fault.

By realizing that my body, like a crystal, is a finely tuned instrument in relationship with everything else, I realized that not only is my anxiety not my fault, it's also not a burden I have to live with my whole life. I used to think that my anxiety was me. It felt all-consuming, like a deep hole I'd never climb out of.

Now I know anxiety is just a tiny part of me—a part of me that is trying to help and support me. By working *with* it (instead of against it), I've "made friends" with it, so to speak. And we're starting to get along really well. I can thank my anxiety for trying to keep me safe, and ultimately release it. Crystals taught me that.

I also share this story because by now, you already know *way* too much about me anyway, and also, it's an important illustration of how crystals, used with intent, can provide benefits on *all* levels.

CONCLUSION

On the basic level of wearing them and keeping them in your pocket, you can gain all kinds of little tidbits of assistance and focus. On the more complicated levels, you can use them in rituals and decision-making for your own personal needs.

Further, you can use them to release trauma on the "tiny" level (like setbacks at work) and on the grander levels (such as a betrayal or a heartbreak). In the case of both, be gentle with yourself.

This PMS experience, overall, taught me a little bit more about myself and my needs (read: I need to be kinder to myself, not just during my time of the month). I hold this with me every day.

And, I hope this book will allow you the same grace. By focusing on specific stress and anxiety needs AND looking at your life more holistically, you can find benefits that not only help you in the moment, but are transformational on every level.

✱

Almost a year after that fateful trip to the crystal shop, my husband and I went to Larissa's annual Christmas party, as usual. Flora was there, of course.

It had been a year of discovery. I'd become a new person in so many ways. I'd gotten a promotion, largely due, I think, to my newfound ability to speak my truth. I'd finished a few stories I'd be working on

CONCLUSION

for a long time. I even submitted one to a prominent magazine... and this time, they seemed interested! The editor said she would get back to me in the new year.

I owed lots of this progress to the self-exploration I'd done as a crystal girl. The crystals themselves helped, of course, but the more important part is who I'd become while learning about them.

My anxiety isn't "cured" by any means, as I think it will always be a part of me. But, it has become something of a side-note, like the color of my eyes or the texture of my hair. I think about it, of course. I just don't stress about it every moment of every single day. Crystals have made sure of that.

On the way to the party, my husband casually mentioned how great it is to see me feeling so much better in general. He is always so supportive during my panicky moments and never complains, even on my worst days. But it's also really tough for him to see me upset, and it can't be easy on him to always need to look after my constant fretting. I always feel like such a burden when I ask for his support, even though he always gives it freely.

His life isn't perfect by any stretch, so I make sure to offer as much support as I can whenever I am able. Since crystals, our relationship has been a bit easier in that aspect. I've been able to offer my

CONCLUSION

husband just as much support as I receive, and it feels really, really good.

It felt exhilarating to talk to him about how much better I'd been feeling lately. It was almost like our relationship had started over, in some ways. Like back when we were first getting to know each other, learning about our deepest selves. He's so supportive of my "crystal habit," and it felt amazing to have him notice the difference.

Although I've been on a crystal journey for a while, I definitely don't see it as coming to an end. I plan on making crystals part of my life for the rest of my life, and I'm excited to see how they shape the course of my journey. None of us can know how our life *might* have been, but I can certainly imagine. I was pretty tired of just getting by, pushing myself through the stress and assuming that my life had to be this way forever.

Instead, I found some simple, fun, and beautiful tools—crystals—that have made all the difference.

I guess the moral of the story is, if your super-cool-edgy-type friend invites you to drinks and the crystal store... do not hesitate. Go! And just see where the road might lead.

Once we got to Larissa's, we got our drinks and mingled with the crowd as usual. I showed Flora the Amethyst ring my husband had bought me as an early Christmas present. (He knows just what I like.)

CONCLUSION

While we were admiring it, Larissa walked over to welcome us to the party. She caught the end of the discussion and started asking about the ring. I started explaining about the Amethyst in the ring, and how—taking a deep breath before nervously continuing—it had some amazing healing properties.

Larissa's eyes widened. "Allegra, you think that ring can actually *heal* stuff?" she asked.

I hesitated again, looking at Flora.

"You've got this one," she said and winked.

THE END

CONCLUSION

REVIEW THE BOOK

The team behind HEALING CRYSTALS FOR THE MIND would be incredibly grateful if you would take 60 seconds to leave a review for our book. Even if it's just a few sentences…

Leave a review at : https://www.amazon.com/review/create-review/?channel=glance-detail&asin=B09CNRVPVP

That link can also be found at: www.AllegraGrant.com

Thank you so much!

CONCLUSION

FREE MINI-BOOK OFFER

In THE COMPLETE GUIDE TO CLEANSING & CHARGING YOUR CRYSTALS, here's what you'll learn:

- Why you should care for your crystals
- A complete guide to Cleansing and Charging Methods
- My personal practices and why I cherish them

Go to www.AllegraGrant.com to get it NOW!

RESOURCES

Beyer, C. (2019). *The Difference Between Magic and Magick*. Learn Religions. https://www.learnreligions.com/magic-and-magick-95856

Chamberlain, L. (2021). Wicca crystal magic: A beginner's guide to practicing Wiccan crystal magic. Sterling Publishing Company.

Conway, D. J. (2010). *The big little book of magick: A Wiccan's guide to altars, candles, pendulums, and healing spells*. Crossing Press.

Frasier, K. (2017). *Crystals for beginners: The guide to get started with the healing power of crystals.* Althea Press.

Hall, J. (2011). *101 power crystals: The ultimate guide to magical crystals, gems, and stones for healing and transformation.* Fair Winds Press.

RESOURCES

Hall, J. (2016). *The crystal Bible: A definitive guide to crystals*. F+W Media.

Jurriaanse, D. (2001). *The practical pendulum book: With instructions for use and 38 pendulum charts*. Red Wheel Weiser.

McCraty, R., & Atkinson, M. (2014). Electrophysiology of intuition: Pre-stimulus responses in group and individual participants using a roulette paradigm. *Global Advances in Health Medicine, 3*(2),16-27. doi:10.7453/gahmj.2014.014

McKusick, E. (2014). *Tuning the human energy field: Healing with vibrational sound therapy*. Healing Arts Press.

Moon, H. (2012). *Crystal grids: How and why they work*. Hibiscus Moon.

Quest, P. (2002). *Reiki for life: The complete guide to Reiki practice for Levels 1, 2, & 3*. Tarcher Perigree.

Rogers, M. (2004). *Breakthrough therapies: Crystal acupuncture and teragram therapy*. AuthorHouse.

Scott, D. E. (2012). *The electric sky: A challenge to the myths of modern astronomy*. Mikamar Publishing.

Van Doren, Y. (2017). *Crystals: The modern guide to crystal healing*. Hardie Grant.

Webster, R. (2002). *Pendulum magic for beginners: Power to achieve all goals*. Llewellyn Publications.

NOTES

INTRODUCTION

1. A quick footnote: Experienced crystal peeps may have guessed what the blue striped rock was: Blue Lace Agate. Flora grinned at me that way at the counter because Blue Lace Agate is a powerful healing crystal that opens you up to honest communication and creativity. It's related to the 5th chakra, located at your throat. She knew my creativity was, figuratively, stuck in my throat. That same crystal is inches away from my keyboard as I type this right now.
2. A footnote to the footnote: I asked Flora if it was okay to mention her in this story, and she filled me in on some other details about her life. What she hadn't told me is that she also has Blue Lace Agate in her collection to help with her creativity—that's why she'd recognized my crystal immediately. It turns out she's been writing erotica for women under a pen name for years, and she's actually kind of famous for it. She doesn't tell people about it because she doesn't want it to be a big deal. Damn, she's so cool.

1. WHAT ARE CRYSTALS, AND DO THEY ACTUALLY WORK?

1. I have routinely thought twice about purchasing pocket-less dresses ever since I started using crystals. Let's just say, if you find a comfy, flattering, gorgeous dress that suits your size and your vibe, *and* it has pockets... do not hesitate. Buy it in every color. You will need it to go with your crystals.
2. I should note here that there are lots of great resources on crystals in the back of this book for you to turn to whenever

you're ready. An excellent crystal resource to get you started is a book called *Crystals For Beginners: The Guide To Get Started with the Healing Power of Crystals* by Karen Frasier. I highly recommend it. Much of my own research began with books and articles by people like Karen, and there is a resource list at the end of this book that explains 1) where I got my info and 2) where you can get the same info for yourself. However, the bulk of my research comes from my own experience–by trying crystals out and seeing how they work for me.

3. Here's an experiment to try: If you want to see an energy field, take an apple seed and cut it in half. Place it on a white background (such as a piece of paper) with the points facing each other, so it looks like a Figure 8. Then, shine a bright light on the apple seed and see if you can notice a faint electric blue halo around it. That's the seed's aura.

    Not everyone can see energy fields, but some people can see them really well, even without doing the apple seed exercise. Do you know anyone who sees colors, perhaps when they have a migraine or they close their eyes to meditate? That's the same gift. (Side note: if you are one of those people, I am wildly jealous of you and your mystical abilities. Please use them for good and perhaps also to look cool in public. Thanks in advance.)

4. There are lots of excellent crystal healing certifications out there if you decide you're really into crystals and want to learn more about them. Some people turn crystal healing into their livelihood, although you could simply use it for extra money or to benefit friends and family. Regardless, getting a certification can just be for fun. It never hurts to have a little extra knowledge, and it's a fun talking point to bring up at parties. If you try a crystal healing class, make sure to find a reputable one with a certified crystal healer.

2. CHOOSING YOUR CRYSTALS

1. Thanks to my therapist, I have learned a little bit about stress and anxiety, and how they're really one-in-the-same, with one difference. Stress is in the present, and anxiety is in the future. If I'm anxious about a phone call tomorrow, I experience stress right now. When people say they are "stressed" about a test tomorrow, "anxious" is really the more accurate word. And when you're feeling stressed, and can't even put your finger on what you're anxious about - oh boy, that's a terrible feeling.

    I say all this to make the point that both terms overlap a great deal, and in this book they sometimes mean the same thing. And sometimes they don't. Don't be too stressed out or anxious about figuring out which is which. They're both problems in your mind, and crystals teach us that we have so much more control over the mind than we ever even imagined. Now, let's back to talking about our feelings.

2. Flora told me it was okay to share this part with you, and she also wants you to know that her traumas have never "gone away," so to speak. They are part of her. But she doesn't carry them like baggage anymore. She wears them like merit badges. Isn't that poetic?

3. Are you saying to yourself, "Um, this is a book about crystals, so why are we talking about charkas?" I can't blame you if you are, but stay with me for a few minutes, and you'll understand why. These are two distinct disciplines, but they complement each other so well. Knowing that you need a third-eye chakra crystal to meditate with before a big meeting, or knowing that Hematite is calling you today because your root chakra is out of balance - well, it'll take your practices up 100 notches. You're welcome to skip to the next chapter to get to the specific crystals, but I promise this section will pay off big if you stick with me.

4. Heart chakra rocks are typically the ones that make me cry, as it so happens. Someone offered to let me hold their new

heart chakra crystals (they were raw Emeralds) because they wanted to show them off and see how I liked their feel. I eagerly grabbed them... and nearly had an emotional meltdown. My friend quickly took them back, and I was able to shake it off in a few seconds. They were too much for me at that moment.

5. Looking back, every teenage attempt I made to stand out by wearing the same rebellious thing everyone else was wearing was just... my throat chakra. I was trying to force my truth instead of just living it. Naturally, if my mom had known this, we would have argued much less about my clothing and hair choices! (At least, that's what I tell myself when I look at cringey pictures in the old yearbooks).

3. 27 CRYSTALS FOR ANXIETY AND STRESS

1. We'll get to best practices when buying crystals at the end of the book, but I'd be remiss if I didn't point out that Malachite, which is very trendy at the moment, is often faked. Real Malachite is actually pretty rare. When you see it in a store, it should be a little more expensive than a pedestrian agate. And, it should feel heavy in your hand, due to the high copper content in the mineral itself. Be careful with this one, friends.
2. Another scam alert! About 75% of the time I see Selenite listed for sale online, it's actually Satin Spar. If you've picked up some Satin Spar do not fret, the properties are very similar. Selenite looks much more like a traditional crystal, and Satin Spar is composed of long sparkly fibers. Again, both are good, but for my money real Selenite is just more powerful.

4. MODERN RITUALS

1. A few months later, in therapy, I came out of the closet as a crystal girl. My therapist immediately went to his desk and pulled out a little keychain with a hunk of citrine in it. He told me he doesn't really believe in crystals, but his wife does. She'd given him the charm, and he loved it because it came from her. Um, are crystals stalking me?!
2. I really want to emphasize this. I've learned that *all* humans are traumatized, at least a tiny bit. There's no such thing as "big" trauma or "small" trauma—we are all traumatized to an extent, and it's all significant to the person who experienced it. But some of us are traumatized *a lot*. And if you are, you need to seek competent help (if you haven't already). Crystals can be really supportive, but they are not a cure-all. Therapy, medication, and whatever else you need to feel okay are exactly what you should do. And if crystals help you in doing these things, so much the better.
3. You may be tempted to have that friend take a picture of you with all your crystals, so you can post it on Instagram. Just be warned, this could have a couple of effects—I know from personal experience. You will definitely get some haters, but you'll probably also find out that you've got some crystal friends you didn't even know you had!
4. Some modern practitioners use the spelling "magick" instead of the standard "magic." There are myriad reasons why, but mostly it's to separate the magick rituals that are the basis of Modern Wicca from the more mundane, David Copperfield version of Vegas magic. Also, adding the "k" means the word has six letters; six is a powerful number to Wiccans.
5. This spell comes from a book called *"Wicca Crystal Magic: A Beginner's Guide to Practicing Wiccan Crystal Magic"* by Lisa Chamberlain. I recommend her entire book for more spells of this kind.

6. A good one is *The Practical Pendulum Book* by D. Jurriaanse, but there are others in the resources list you can check out.
7. I have definitely gotten weird wiggly-shaped answers that meant "meh," or "I don't know, you choose!" which are always so frustrating to the stress-ridden mind. That's why keeping it simple is better. I used to try to make *all* my decisions with my pendulum, but that was merely feeding my anxiety instead of helping it. Not to mention, it took up so much time. I learned to work *with* my pendulum, not use it as some kind of mystical, all-knowing oracle.
8. Forgive me for the ten problematic things I just said about this process, as I firmly believe gender is a construct, and the gender binary is an entirely incomplete way to look at identity. But this was the 1950s; they just didn't have the vocabulary yet.
9. I keep meaning to use elixir water in the base of my Christmas tree, but I forget every year. I'll do it this year and report back!

5. USING CRYSTALS TO SOOTHE YOUR STRESS AND ANXIETY

1. A good release, like a cry, a laugh—or, frankly, an orgasm—is a great way to reset all your energies. <<blush>>
2. I have also found that fatigue is sometimes due to other people's negative energy staying trapped in my aura. By using a crystal elixir spray or passing a Selenite wand through my aura, I can actually lift quite a bit of fatigue instantly. If you're feeling really worn out, try this and see. It could be that you've been around some angsty people lately, and their energy is sticking to you. It's like dragging around a bag of bricks with you all day—an obviously exhausting thing to do.
3. If your subconscious *is* telling you that whatever you're doing isn't in alignment with your highest and best good,

don't panic! Make a mental note of the information, and later on (when you've finished your task), take some meditative journaling time to figure out why the task wasn't in your best interest.

Your anxiety is just trying to protect you, after all. So if the task is something you can pay someone else to do or cut out of your life completely, do it. There's no shame in automating your life. We have so many modern conveniences these days, so if you just can't focus on cooking or cleaning or eating or taxes or organizing spreadsheets or whatever it is, find another way to do it, so you don't have to. Sometimes, my intuition has told me that I couldn't focus on a task because it just wasn't where I wanted to go in my career or my life, so I found a way to change my life path accordingly. The lesson here is that sometimes we think we have to do certain things, but we really, *really* don't. Do only what you truly desire to do. Let the rest go—as much as you can safely do so without ruining your career or relationships or whatever. That stuff is important and sometimes has to come first. Just not *all* the time. You come first sometimes, too.

6. CARING FOR YOURSELF AND YOUR CRYSTALS

1. Although, now that I think about it, I bought a bag of random stones on Amazon for $18, and it gave me a piece of Red Jasper that has become a treasured piece of my collection. So, you never know!
2. These are the same bags I mentioned in Chapter 4 for use as crystal "charm bags."
3. I know, it's so tempting to wear that new bracelet home from the shop or all day at the festival. If you want to do this, ask the seller if they have recently charged their crystals or can charge them right then. Some Reiki healers, for

instance, can charge the crystals with Reiki in a few milliseconds, which is nice. Regardless, you don't want the energy of any other customers who might have handled the crystals before you to stay on your newly purchased treasures. If you're out and about and want to pour some water from your water bottle on your new crystals to cleanse them, that can be a nice option. If anyone judges you, smile blandly at them and offer them a crystal. Perhaps they need some Kyanite to work on their judginess!